Navigating the Information Tsunami: Engaging Research Projects that Meet the Common Core State Standards, K-5

Edited by Kristin Fontichiaro

CHERRY LAKE PUBLISHING • ANN ARBOR, MICHIGAN

HOW STANDARDS ARE USED IN THIS BOOK

Each lesson in this book addresses one or more standards from the K–5 Common Core State Standards (CCSS — http://corestandards.org). We refer to these as key standards, and their scope is often general. For example, standard Writing 2.7 reads, "Participate in shared research and writing projects (e.g., read a number of books on a single topic to produce a report; record science observations)." This standard identifies an activity (e.g., participate, read, or record) but does not articulate what kinds of additional skills students must have to complete that activity (e.g., formulate questions, navigate a text, locate information, and take notes).

As experienced teachers of research, we recognize the need to identify, articulate, and teach those "hidden" skills. Therefore, each lesson in this book begins by identifying the CCSS standard(s). Underneath, in the section marked, "To achieve this standard, students will need to be able to," we list the necessary building-block :sub-skills." In some cases, these are taken directly from the CCSS. If so, they are cited as such. If an item in this list is not cited, then it is not found explicitly in the CCSS even though it is an essential skill for achieving the key standard.

Special thanks to Martika Allen, Jen Colby, Kara Fribley, Amanda Kauffman, Emily Johnson, Shauna Masura, Jill Morningstar, Natalie Mulder, and Samantha Roslund for their feedback.

The contributors to this book have donated their fees to the Spectrum Scholars Fund of the American Library Association.

Photo Credits: Cover and page 1, ©Kalenik Hanna/Shutterstock, Inc.; page 8, ©Zoltan Pataki/Shutterstock, Inc.; page 36, ©Francesco Dazzi/Shutterstock, Inc.; page 81 (left), Arthur Rothstein/National Archives; page 81 (top right), Arthur Rothstein/Library of Congress; page 81 (bottom right), Dorothea Lange/Library of Congress.

Standards quoted in this book are © 2010 by National Governors Association Center for Best Practices and Council of Chief State School Officers. All rights reserved. More information about the Common Core State Standards is available at *www.corestandards.org*.

4972 7067   11/12

Table of Contents

Introduction

Kristin Fontichiaro

Welcome to this collection of lesson plans that brings together the Common Core State Standards (CCSS) and research projects for grades K–5. If you've picked up this book, it's probably because you are an educator in one of the 46 states that have, as of this publication, adopted the CCSS for English Language Arts and Math.

The CCSS is an initiative led by the National Governors Association Center for Best Practices and the Council of Chief State School Officers. The intent of CCSS is to provide more consistent learning outcomes across state lines and to raise the level of challenge and rigor for all students, whether they are college- or workforce-bound. Each state decided independently whether they wanted to join CCSS or keep their existing state standards, so if your state legislators adopted Common Core, your local district must participate.

If you work in a CCSS-adopting state, your state standardized test will be replaced by a computerized assessment. Each state joined either the Partnership for assessment of Readiness for College and Careers (PARCC, www.parcconline.org/about-parcc) or Smarter Balanced (www.k12.wa.us/smarter) consortia, and each consortia is developing a multistate computerized assessment. This means your students will be compared not only to other students in your state, but also to students in any of the consortia's partner states.

What Is the Difference Between Standards and Curriculum?

The CCSS are standards, not curriculum. At each grade level, the CCSS list the exit outcomes or, in other words, what things students should know and demonstrate skill in. The CCSS do not mandate how you teach students to reach those outcomes. They simply give educators the finish line that all students are expected to cross. We hope you'll use the lessons in this book to help you think in new ways about how you can meet the research-related CCSS.

What Can This Book Help With?

We believe in great research opportunities for kids in the digital age. Thirty years ago, it could take hours to find the information that today's students—even our youngest, whose fingers tentatively reach for each keystroke—can find in moments. Today's abundant digital resources mean we no longer need to restrict our students to reciting found facts. In an era of informational abundance, we can help our students springboard into deeper and more resonant learning that, along the way, is more fun, more engaging, and more compelling for students and teachers. But don't worry: each of these lessons can be accomplished with print or digital resources, or a combination!

The contributors to this book were selected for their thoughtful approaches to research. Like you, they have realized that many of the standards—such as Writing 3.7 ("Conduct short research projects that build knowledge about a topic")—seem simple on the surface but, upon further reflection, provoke more questions than answers. What goes into conducting a short research project? What does it mean to build knowledge? In each lesson, the authors will unpack the CCSS standard into the numerous smaller skills (sometimes explicit CCSS standards, sometimes implicit) that go into that standard. They'll share their favorite teaching books, Web sites, and paid online resources, and walk you through lessons that will help you guide students from engagement to note taking to synthesis and a final product.

What Comprises a Good Research Project?

There are many well-known research models and processes. You may already be familiar with the Big6 (www.big6.com) or the Stripling Model of Inquiry (see http://tps.govst.edu/pdfs/StriplingModelInquiry.pdf). Regardless of your district's preferred model, all research practices are iterative, not linear. We don't move automatically from one phase to the next without turning back. Great research raises new questions, sending us back and forth between stages of the process. In general, however, research projects consider these phases:

- *Connecting to or building prior knowledge.* Students need a framework upon which new learning can be built. Showing students how something they already know connects to something new helps builds lasting understanding. In this book, watch for prior knowledge strategies, such as brainstorming, reading a text, viewing a film, or exploring an object.
- *Developing questions.* One of the hallmarks of a curious learner—and elementary students are the most curious of all!—is the ability to develop and explore questions. In this book, you will see a gradual transition from teacher-guided to student-guided questions, as well as some reinforcement about what comprises better questions. We want students to go beyond finding factual answers and to realize that the research habits they are learning in school can apply equally to their real lives.
- *Identifying and navigating great resources.* As adults, we have years of reading comprehension and evaluation strategies to help us select great resources. This is much harder for elementary students, who often lack content understanding or linguistic nuances.

Oftentimes, our students' digital fearlessness means they will use search engines with gusto…but with little expertise! Many of the lessons in this book pre-identify effective resources, although a mini-lesson on constructing better Web searches (pages 93 and 94) meets students where they are. And books still count!

- *Taking or making notes.* Extracting useful information from a source takes a lot of practice. Graphic organizers can help students think through the information they want to use instead of merely cutting and pasting from a resource and into their product.
- *Sorting and sequencing notes to synthesize and find meaning.* As students move into the upper elementary grades, they need more independent practice at sorting their notes and putting them in a meaningful order.
- *Creating a product to communicate what students have learned.* The lessons in this book each include a product at the conclusion of research, either digital or handmade.
- *Assessing the process and product.* Helping students to look critically at their work process (e.g., efficiency, note-taking skills, reading skills) and the product (e.g., neatness, aesthetics, expressiveness, writing skills) helps them sit in the driver's seat of their learning.

Does Every Research Project Have to Include Every Step?

In many cases, you may find that making a product will consume a week of time that you cannot afford to spend. Don't be afraid to make one or two steps the focus of your lesson. For example, you could plan a research activity that stops with note-taking and, in lieu of creating a project, concludes with students discussing what they have learned with one another. These sharing conversations not only help students formulate what they have learned but can help them meet the Speaking and Listening strand of CCSS. However, do not truncate steps where students are engaging in the kinds of critical thinking, synthesis, and understanding that are the heart of the CCSS movement—we can't cut note-taking in order to make a slide show!

The Tinkertoy Approach

As of this book's publication, only the English Language Arts and Math standards have been released. Science and Social Studies standards are still in development. This means that, district by district and state by state, there is no consistency in what content is taught at which grade level. As a result, we encourage you to consider the lesson plans not only for your grade level, but also for a grade above or below. If your fifth graders study Manifest Destiny and not the Dust Bowl, as in Melissa Johnston's lesson on page 79, swap out one topic for another. As you would with Tinkertoys, feel free to deconstruct, mash up, and build your own variations.

Am I in This Alone?

No! The standards also do not mandate who must teach the standards. We strongly encourage classroom teachers to partner with reading specialists, librarians, special education consultants, literacy and math coaches, and other staff. Teaching great research takes a lot of energy. Partner teaching means you halve the student-teacher ratio and can provide more intensive feedback to the students who need it. Plus, you gain a partner who can help you observe, plan, think, and assess!

So let's get started. Let's tame the information tsunami and help our elementary students build a solid set of research and writing skills. Dive in!

Kindergarten

HOW DO WE KNOW WHAT WOOLLY MAMMOTHS WERE LIKE IF THEY DON'T EXIST ANYMORE?

Keywords: prehistoric times, mammoths, primary sources, learning with objects
Kristin Fontichiaro

Kindergarteners are ideal researchers. They love to think, learn, discuss, and share. Teachers can harness this enthusiasm when they engage in research projects that do not require the teacher to mediate between student and resource. In this lesson, students use hands-on exploration and a multimedia resource in lieu of hearing a book read aloud, in order to create questions and gather information. The final product is a collaborative piece of writing, drawing, and/or dictation.

Key Standard

Writing K.2—Use a combination of drawing, dictating, and writing to compose informative/explanatory texts in which they name what they are writing about and supply some information about the topic.

To achieve this standard, students will need to be able to

- with prompting and support, ask and answer questions about key details in a text (Reading Informational Text K.1);
- actively engage in group reading activities with purpose and understanding (Reading Informational Text K.10);
- participate in collaborative discussions with diverse partners about kindergarten topics and texts, with peers and adults in small and larger groups (Speaking and Listening K.1);
- add drawings or other visual displays to descriptions as desired, to provide additional detail (Speaking and Listening K.5); and
- speak audibly and express thoughts, feelings, and ideas clearly (Speaking and Listening K.6).

Time Needed

Two 30- to 40-minute sessions

Resource List

- ☑ Chart paper divided into three columns, labeled "See," "Think," and "Wonder"
- ☑ Markers for chart paper
- ☑ Drawing software (e.g., Microsoft Paint, Kid Pix, or TuxPaint) or paper and markers/crayons/colored pencils, for writing and illustrating a class book page
- ☑ Mammoth tooth hidden inside a pillowcase or tote bag (borrow from your local natural history museum or environmental center)
- ☑ PebbleGo Animals database (PebbleGo.com) with headphones and computers, or:
  - *Woolly Mammoths* by Helen Frost (Capstone/Pebble Plus, 2006)
  - *Mammoths on the Move* by Lisa Wheeler, illustrated by Kurt Cyrus (Harcourt, 2006)
  - *Find Out Firsthand: Using Primary Sources* by Kristin Fontichiaro (Cherry Lake, 2013)

Base of a mastadon tooth

DAY ONE (40 minutes): Research
Launching the Lesson: Activating Prior Knowledge

1. Ask kindergarteners to sit in a circle. Start by saying, "Today, we will be learning about something from a very long time ago. I have it in my bag. The first thing I want us all to do is pass around this secret item."

2. Pull the mammoth tooth out and say, "As you pass it around, tell us what you see or feel. Even if you think you know what it is, keep it a secret and don't tell! Just describe what you see when you look at it or what it feels like in your hands."

3. Students pass around the tooth, sharing their observations. Common responses may include "heavy," "ridges," "brown," "big," "oval," or comparison phrases such as "bigger than my foot." The instructor scribes these in the first column on the chart paper.

4. Say, "Those are all really interesting words. If I closed my eyes and heard those words, it would be easy for me to imagine that object in my mind. Now let's move to another question. What do you think this object might be? Turn and talk to the person sitting next to you. I'll count down from five to zero when it's time to stop talking and share with the group."

5. Students chat with one another.

6. Say, "5-4-3-2-1-0 noise. Good job, everybody. Who heard an idea they really liked?"

7. Students share their ideas. The teacher scribes them. Common responses are that it is a foot, a rock, or a stone.

8. Say, "Great thinking! Those are all good guesses. Scientists have studied these for many years, and they can tell us that this is actually...a tooth! A really big tooth from an animal that doesn't live on Earth anymore. It's the tooth from a woolly mammoth, like you have been studying in class! I have one more question. Now that you know this is a woolly mammoth tooth, what do you wonder about this tooth? Wonderings are questions. I'll start. My question is, "If this is how big the tooth was, how big was the mammoth? Turn and talk to your neighbor. I'll count down when it's time to stop."

9. Students talk in pairs. Say, "5-4-3-2-1-0 noise. Good job, everybody. Let's share some of our favorite wonderings." The instructor records them on chart paper.

Learning Activities

1. Say, "Now we're going to go to the computers. You will see that they are on the PebbleGo screen—and that animal is a woolly mammoth. Use the arrows to move from screen to screen. Wear headphones so you can hear them read the words out loud to you. After you finish, we'll make a new chart paper listing what you learned."

2. Students navigate the woolly mammoth content. They then move to stations (in a library, this may include browsing or checking out books; in a classroom, this may include quiet reading or moving to regular centers). One station/center is the chart paper station, where students share what they have learned with an adult who writes or helps them record their answer. If their answer answers something from the Wonder column, note that. Record images as well as words, as time permits.

DAY TWO (30 minutes): Writing
Launching the Lesson: Activating Prior Knowledge

1. Read aloud the chart paper from the day before. Say, "We have learned a lot about woolly mammoths! We should share this information with other people like the principal, the librarian, or your parents. Mario is passing out a piece of paper to each person. At the top of the paper, you're going to draw a picture of the most interesting thing you learned. Underneath, you will write, or we will help you write, the words that tell what you learned. I'll show you my sample, but I know you'll want to write something different so our book has a lot of different ideas in it."

2. Model a sample on the board, showing how sentences begin with a capital letter and end with a period.

3. Technology alternative: Ask each student to create a page using software like Kid Pix. Combine them into a slide show.

Learning Activities

Students create their pages, which are eventually bound into a class book or collected into a digital class slide show.

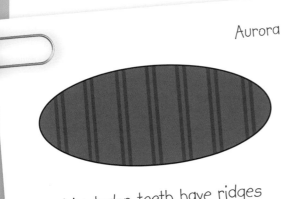

Aurora

Mastodon teeth have ridges to help them chew plants.

Closure Read aloud the class book or slide show. Discuss with students what they learned about mastodons and about using books (or the computer) to learn about things from long ago.

Assessment Instructors will chat and give informal feedback throughout the process. A successful product will include a drawing that the student can discuss with the instructor, and will feature a dictated or written sentence that reflects accurate content.

Extensions With the school librarian, use one of the additional texts in the Resources section to extend the students' knowledge. Continue to add to the See-Think-Wonder chart over time. Think of other objects or images, following this method, that you can use to introduce new concepts or themes in literature, social studies, or science. A seed growing in a transparent plastic cup, a firefighter's flashlight, or an antique children's book can all trigger fascinating conversations.

WHAT CAN TOMIE DEPAOLA TEACH US ABOUT BEING A GOOD AUTHOR?

Keywords: author study, Tomie dePaola, habits of writers, literature

Jenny Harner

Sharing examples of quality writing is one way to help young writers develop good writing skills early. One suggestion authors share is to "write what you know." Tomie dePaola often uses moments in his life as inspiration for his books. In this series of lessons, students are exposed to several of Tomie's works. In addition to studying his literature, students focus on what good writers do and how Tomie demonstrates those traits.

Key Standard

Writing K.7—Participate in shared research and writing projects (e.g., explore a number of books by a favorite author and express opinions about them).

To achieve this standard, students will need to be able to

- with prompting and support, ask and answer questions about key details in a text (Reading Literature K.1);
- name the author and illustrator of a text, and define the role of each in telling the story (Reading Literature K.6);
- actively engage in group reading activities with purpose and understanding (Reading Literature K.10); and
- with prompting and support, describe the connection between two individuals, events, ideas, or pieces of information in a text (Reading Informational Text K.3).

Time Needed

Time before unit for reading; two 40-minute sessions for activity

Resource List

- ☑ A wide variety of Tomie dePaola books, including one or more biographies (check with your librarian for multiple copies of titles)
- ☑ Chart paper divided into three columns titled: "What Tomie's Books Are About," "What Good Authors Do," and "How Tomie's Life Helped Him Become a Good Author"
- ☑ Class set of book page copies

DAYS LEADING UP TO LAUNCH OF UNIT

Launching the Lesson: Activating Prior Knowledge

1. Ask your librarian to provide you with a wide selection of Tomie dePaola books.
2. Invite the class to sit in the story area and share with them the books from the librarian.
3. Explain, "Our librarian has brought us a huge basket of books to enjoy! Each book in this basket was written by the same author. His name is Tomie dePaola. Tomie is an interesting author because although some of his stories come from his imagination, he writes other books about memories he has from being a kid like you! I'm going to hand these books out. I'd like you to take a picture walk through one of the books with someone sitting near you. When you do a picture walk, you turn to each picture in the book, looking for clues about what the book could be about."
4. After passing out books to partners and letting students enjoy their picture walks ask, "What types of stories do you think we'll be reading? What did you see in your books?" As students share what they saw in their stories, record their responses on chart paper under the heading "What Tomie Writes About."
5. Explain, "Over the next couple of weeks, we are going to read many of these books by Tomie dePaola. As we read and enjoy them, we are also going to talk about what good writers do. That will help us become good writers, too."

Learning Activities

Over a two-week period, spend time reading several Tomie dePaola books. Each time you read, allow a student to select a book from the basket for the class to share. At the conclusion of each book, have a discussion including questions such as, "What was this story about? What are some qualities of good writers that Tomie showed us today? Was this a story based on Tomie's life or one from his imagination? How can you tell?"

Record student ideas on chart paper under "What Tomie Writes About" and "What Good Writers Do." When recording things good writers do, have students share examples from the stories. Ensure that the books are available before and after they are read as a whole group, so students can preview or revisit them.

Closure Summarize the conversation for the students.

Assessment Observation and notes made on chart paper will help you know the level of the students' understanding.

DAY ONE (40 minutes): Exploration: How does life help us write better? Launching the Lesson: Activating Prior Knowledge

1. Begin with the chart paper that students have added to over the last two weeks and share, "We have spent a lot of time reading Tomie dePaola's books recently. Our chart is full of information about what Tomie writes about and what good writers do."
2. Read a few student comments aloud.

Learning Activities

1. Say, "Today, we're going to read a biography about Tomie's life. A biography is a book that tells us the story of someone's real life. Let's see if we can find anything in this book to help us understand how his life experiences helped Tomie become a good writer." Read one of dePaola's autobiographical books (e.g., *Nana Upstairs & Nana Downstairs*).
2. After reading, ask students, "How do you think Tomie's life experiences helped him become a good writer?"
3. Allow them to turn and talk to their neighbor about their ideas.
4. Then, as students share their ideas, record them on the chart paper under "How Tomie's Life Helped Him Become a Good Author." Help students understand that while some of his life experiences gave him ideas for books like *The Art Lesson*, other experiences helped his imagination grow or let Tomie know that he had supportive teachers and parents who wanted him to be his best.

Closure Summarize the day's conversation.

Assessment Observation and notes made on chart paper will help you know the level of the students' understanding.

DAY TWO (40 minutes): Writing
Launching the Lesson: Activating Prior Knowledge

1. Explain to the students, "Today, we're going to create a class book about what Tomie dePaola has taught us about being good writers. We're going to share our book with the librarian to show her everything we learned from the books she lent us. Let's look at our chart again."
2. Review the notes that students have collected about Tomie.

Learning Activities

1. Continue with, "You're going to write about one thing good writers do. Then, you're going to find a place in a book where Tomie showed us how good writers show that trait. You will write it on your page, and at the end, we'll take all of our writing and turn it into a class book. This book will help us as we begin to do our own writing. I have an example page to show you. (Show a projection of your sample.) One thing good writers do is use good spelling. Tomie showed us this in his book *Stagestruck* when he made sure all the words were spelled right. I'm sure you have lots of other, more creative ideas! I'm going to give you some time to talk to your table groups and see how many different ideas you can come up with."
2. Circulate among students and help them record their ideas. Rather than asking students to illustrate their responses, take photographs of the students holding up the Tomie dePaola book they wrote about and print the photographs for the bottom of each writing page. Either bind the pages into a book or scan the pages to create a digital slide show.

Closure Invite your librarian to your classroom to share the class book or slide show. Have students review what they learned about things good writers do and how Tomie showed those traits. Ensure the book or slide show is easily accessible so students can use it as reference as they begin to create more of their own writing.

Assessment A successful product will include something that good writers do and an example from a Tomie dePaola book.

Extensions Encourage students to write stories using events in their own lives as inspiration.

Name _____

One thing good writers do is _____

_____

_____

Tomie showed us this in his book _____

_____

_____

when he _____

_____

_____

From Navigating the Information Tsunami: Engaging Research Projects That Meet the Common Core State Standards, K-5. Cherry Lake Publishing, 2013.

WHAT SHAPES CAN WE FIND IN OUR ENVIRONMENT THAT ARE NATURAL OR MADE BY HUMANS?

Keywords: shapes, photography, slide shows, podcasting

Jenny Harner

Students in kindergarten are constantly becoming more aware of their environment and their place in it. This lesson asks them to look more closely at the world around them and make real-world connections to basic shape identification in math class. By creating digital products, students can "write" with their voice, which gives them a stronger opportunity to share what they know and understand.

Key Standard

Writing K.8—With guidance and support from adults, recall information from experiences or gather information from provided sources to answer a question.

To achieve this standard, students will need to be able to

- describe objects in the environment using names of shapes, and describe the relative positions of these objects using terms such as "above," "below," "beside," "in front of," "behind," and "next to" (Math K.G.1);
- correctly name shapes, regardless of their orientations or overall size (Math K.G.2);
- participate in collaborative discussions with diverse partners about kindergarten topics and texts, with peers and adults in small and larger groups (Speaking and Listening K.1);
- speak audibly and express thoughts, feelings, and ideas clearly (Speaking and Listening K.6);
- actively engage in group reading activities with purpose and understanding (Reading Informational Text K.10); and
- identify parts of their environment that are man-made or are natural.

Time Needed

Four 30-minute sessions

Resource List

- ☑ Shoe boxes with plain 2-D and 3-D shapes for each group (squares, circles, triangles, rectangles, hexagons, cubes, cones, cylinders, and spheres)
- ☑ Shape books, e.g.:
  - *Shapes Everywhere* by Cecilia Minden (Cherry Lake, 2011)
  - *The Shape of Things* by Dayle Ann Dodds (Candlewick, 1996)
  - *Shapes, Shapes, Shapes* by Tana Hoban (Greenwillow, 1996)
- ☑ Photographs of shapes in the world, from personal or Creative Commons photo collection (e.g., http://flickrcc.bluemountains.net)
- ☑ Digital cameras
- ☑ Podcast creation software such as Photo Story for PC (free download: www.microsoft.com/download/en/details.aspx?id=11132) or GarageBand for Mac
- ☑ A sample podcast

DAY ONE (30 minutes): Shapes
Launching the Lesson: Activating Prior Knowledge

1. Start by saying, "Recently, we've been working on identifying all types of shapes. I would like you to open the shoe box on your table and work with your group to review the names of all the different shapes we've learned."
2. After giving them a few moments to work together, ask a few students to share shapes they identified.

3. Continue by saying, "For the next few classes, we're going to be looking for these shapes in our environment. When I look at the rectangle in our boxes, I also realize that's the shape of a book, our door, and the window. What other things do you think of when you look at the shapes in your boxes?"
4. Allow students to brainstorm ideas. Provide titles from the Resource List to aid in brainstorming.

Learning Activities

1. Project a photograph on the screen and share, "This is a photograph I took on vacation. Take a moment to investigate the environment in this image. What shapes do you see?"
2. Give them some time to think and look at the details of the pictures. Ask for a volunteer. "Mike, can you come up to the board and highlight or outline a shape you have identified?"
3. After the student identifies the shape say, "Good job, Mike. I see a cylinder there, too! Can you explain how you know it is a cylinder?" Also ask, "Based on what we've learned in science, do you think that is a natural or man-made part of this environment? How do you know?"
4. Allow several students to identify and explain the shapes they find in the photographs.

Closure Share that in the coming days, the class is going to go on a shape hunt and take pictures of shapes in their world.

Assessment Observation of student responses will give the opportunity for instantaneous formative feedback.

DAY TWO (30 minutes per group): Photography
Launching the Lesson: Activating Prior Knowledge
Remind students of the previous lesson's activities.

Learning Activities

1. Explain, "Today we're going to explore our environment and use digital cameras to take pictures of shapes we find. Our librarian has several cameras with her that she's going to share with us."
2. Allow the librarian to share a few quick pointers about using the digital cameras. Emphasize the importance of carrying the camera by using its wrist or neck strap so it can't fall off by accident!
3. Split the classroom into smaller groups so that the librarian, the classroom teacher, and an aide/paraprofessional/volunteer each have a group. (This could also be organized so that the librarian works with a group during centers or reading group time over one or several days.)
4. Within each group, have the adult ask, "Where do you think we could go looking for shapes today?" As students brainstorm ideas, the adult can write them down.
5. Next, the adult can bring the small group of children around the school and playground looking for shapes to photograph. As the group arrives at different locations, ask students to identify shapes they see in the area.
6. Once they have identified shapes, allow students to take a photograph. Ensure that each student takes a picture. (Tip: After each student takes a photograph, check to be certain it is focused—young photographers often move more quickly than their camera's shutter!—and have the teacher or another student take the photographer's picture next. That way, you'll be sure to know whose photograph is whose.)

Closure Thank the students for their work and let them know that their images will be moved from their cameras to the computers for the next session.

Assessment Observation and conversation will give the adults a sense of the students' understanding. Between Days One and Two, work with the librarian to import the digital images into the software. Also, work with the librarian to make a sample recording of an adult explaining the shapes in a photograph as well as identifying which shapes are man-made and which are natural. Print a small copy of each picture for the student photographers to use as they decide what to say in their podcast.

DAY THREE (10 minutes per student): Adding Technology
Launching the Lesson: Activating Prior Knowledge

Say to students, "Remember when we walked around, inside and outside the school, looking for shapes and taking pictures? We've been getting those photos ready for the next step of your project!"

Learning Activities

1. Explain to students, "Today we are going to create a podcast. You're going to be able to share the photographs you took and record your voices explaining the shapes you found. Here is an example that the librarian and I made."

2. Continue with, "We are going to give you a small printout of the photograph you took last time. When you get your photograph, find the shapes you identified when you took the picture. Also look at the rest of the picture. Do you see any more shapes hiding in there?"

3. After giving students their printed photograph, give them a few moments to look for additional shapes they may have missed while focusing on the main object.

4. Then ask them to turn and talk to the person next to them about the shapes in their picture. After they've shared, continue with, "Finally, after you see your shapes and explain them to your partner, decide which objects are man-made and which ones are natural. Tell your partner after you decide."

5. Explain, "The librarian will work with one student at a time at the computer. When you sit with her, she will ask you to explain the shapes in your picture. Don't forget to mention if your shapes are man-made or natural! You'll be talking into a microphone so that we can listen to your explanation later." Give the students another task to work on while the recording is going on. This will maximize engagement and minimize background noise.
   (The lesson may stop here for the day or continue, as time allows.)

Closure Say, "Great job, everyone! Tomorrow, we'll have our premiere and watch everyone's recording!"

Assessment Feedback is given as each student records. Students needing more time or additional attempts are coached by the librarian as needed.

DAY FOUR (30 minutes): Viewing Final Products
Launching the Lesson: Activating Prior Knowledge

Watch the podcast as a class. Before watching and listening, ask the students to be thinking about a compliment to share with a classmate. Also ask them to think about how their next podcast could be even better.

Assessment A successful product will be an accurate, oral explanation of their photograph including shapes and whether those shapes are man-made or natural.

Extensions Students could use shapes to create illustrations, then use that artwork as inspiration for future writing. Think about other opportunities to bring podcasting into your classroom. Allowing young students to verbalize their answers can help them extend and explain their thinking.

Grade 1

WHAT MAKES AN ANIMAL UNIQUE?

Keywords: animals, questioning, podcasting, animation
Linda Martin

First graders continue to develop reading skills. They are excited researchers who, with prompting and support, can transfer factual information from a text to an organizer to a cohesive narrative. In this lesson, students utilize their natural curiosity and sociability to share information about animals in an animated presentation.

Key Standard

Writing 1.2—Write informative/explanatory texts in which they name a topic, supply some facts about the topic, and provide some sense of closure.

To achieve this standard, students will need to be able to

- read with sufficient accuracy and fluency to support comprehension (from Reading Fluency 1.4);
- use the illustrations and details in a text to describe its key ideas (Reading Informational Text 1.7);
- make notes; and
- use technology to share learning.

Resource List

- ☑ An assortment of print materials on various animals (books, magazines, encyclopedias); ask the school librarian
- ☑ Chart paper and markers, whiteboard, or interactive board for group planning
- ☑ Graphic organizer (made after Day One)
- ☑ Attribute table for differentiation
- ☑ Animal photographs (try www.flickr.com/creativecommons or netTrekker.com); put a few images of each animal in a shared drive folder or on the desktop of the students' computers
- ☑ Free Blabberize.com account
- ☑ Computers with microphones
- ☑ Scrap paper and pencils

Time Needed

Seven 45-minute sessions

DAY ONE (45 minutes): Selecting an Animal to Research
Launching the Lesson: Activating Prior Knowledge

1. Set a wide assortment of appropriate level animal books on tables or desks. You might add a visual prop (e.g., a stuffed animal, deerstalker hat, or magnifying glass) as an attention-getter.
2. Say, "Raise your hand if you want to be a detective. Great! Now raise your hand if you like animals. Wonderful! We are going on a detective search for clues about animals. We will learn about them, then teach each other. We will use the helping tools in informational books. Remember how we use the table of contents and the index to find facts in our informational books? We will use them to find facts about animals for this project."
3. "Now we are going to the tables to look at the animal books. Look at all of the books. Open them up. See which ones are interesting. When you have looked at all of them, decide which animal you want to research. Take that book and return to the carpet. I will make a list with your name and animal so we know who is writing about which animal."

Learning Activities

1. After everyone has an animal book and is gathered back together, say, "Now that you have an animal to research, let's decide what you want to find out. Turn to your neighbor and take turns telling one another what questions you have about your animal."
2. Give the students a few minutes to talk and share ideas in pairs. Call them back together. Ask the students to share their questions with the class. List the questions on chart paper or on the board.
3. Say, "Wow. We have a lot of questions! Do you see any questions that are alike or can be grouped together?" If students need prompting, suggest a topic such as habitat—e.g., "How many questions ask about an animal's home, habitat, or where it lives?" As students find topics of interest, list them on the board (e.g., habitat, appearance, diet). Suggest the catch-all category "interesting facts" for questions that do not fit elsewhere.

Closure Say, "Now we have an animal to learn about and questions that we want to find answers to. Tomorrow, we will put on our detective hats and search for those answers! Now that you have heard everyone else's questions, have you thought of any new questions? Turn to your neighbor and share." After a few minutes, let a few students share their new questions with the group.

Assessment Observe student conversations and read over their questions for insight into students' understanding. Convert their questions into a graphic organizer and make a copy for each student.

DAY TWO (45 minutes): Research and Note Taking
Launching the Lesson: Activating Prior Knowledge

1. Say, "Today, you will look for clues about your animals in your book. Remember that you do not have to write down everything in a paragraph. You are looking for just the few words that answer your questions. This is when your detective skills come in. The words that answer your questions are your clues. I'll show you first, then we'll practice together for a bit to make sure everyone knows what to do."
2. Show a paragraph on a PowerPoint slide about an animal and model how you would take notes using as few words as possible. Next, show a second paragraph for students to practice with. Circulate throughout the group, giving feedback. After five minutes, go to the next slide, which has the paragraph with the keywords in a different color from the rest of the paragraph. As you point out each keyword, ask students to raise their hands if they have that word on their paper.

Learning Activities

1. Say, "Now open your books while I pass out the graphic organizers. Use your informational text features to look for clues and answers to your questions. Write your keywords in the appropriate section of your organizer. If you have any questions, raise your hand and I will help you."
2. As students work, check in with individuals or small groups to make sure the note taking is progressing smoothly.

Closure Call students together. Ask, "What was the most difficult part of finding clues? Who has a hint to make the process easier?" Let students share their strategies.

Assessment Collect the student organizers for feedback. Review them and make a list of students who would benefit from a note-taking mini-conference.

DAY THREE (45 minutes): Research and Note Taking
Launching the Lesson: Activating Prior Knowledge

Repeat Day Two's note-taking exercise with a fresh text. After three minutes, go to the next slide, which has the paragraph with the keywords underlined or in a different color from the rest of the paragraph. As you point out each keyword, ask students to raise their hands if they wrote that word on their paper. Their papers will act as a mini-assessment for their note-taking progress.

Learning Activities Students will continue to take notes from their sources. Some students will move quickly through their material and may use multiple sources. Students who have difficulty picking out the important facts might benefit from an attribute table. The table below will help them focus their reading as they check off the attributes that fit their animal.

My Animal by _____

	Habitat		Appearance							Diet		
	Land	Water	2 Feet	4 Feet	Wings	Fur	Feathers	Fins	Horns	Plants	Insects	Animals
Frogs	✘	✘		✘							✘	

Closure Ask students to reflect on what was challenging or successful for them today.

DAY FOUR (45 minutes): Writing
Launching the Lesson: Activating Prior Knowledge

1. Say, "Today, you should almost be through with your note-taking. Now you will move on to the next step in the writing process and turn your notes into sentences. Can you write a sentence or two from each section of your graphic organizer? Let's do one together. Here is my graphic organizer about lions. I have words like 'meat,' 'mammals,' 'fur,' and 'live babies.' So I might write: Lions eat meat. They are mammals. They have fur and live babies.

2. "After you write some sentences about your animal, think about how you can introduce and end your report. Let's play around with some opening and closing ideas." Model them on the board, e.g., "Have you ever wanted to know about lions?" and "Now you know all about lions!"

Learning Activities As students work, conference with small groups and individuals. Help them organize and write their thoughts.

Closure Bring the group back together. "How did today go? Who wrote something they want to share?" Sometimes, at this stage of the note-taking process, young researchers get tired. Leave them with a feeling of excitement and anticipation: "Tomorrow, we will do something really fun with the paragraphs we are writing. I cannot wait to show you!"

DAY FIVE (45 minutes): Writing and Technology
Launching the Lesson: *Activating Prior Knowledge*

Say, "We are almost finished with our sentences and paragraphs. Let's keep working, using yesterday's notes from the board to help. At the end of the lesson, I will show you a fun way we can teach each other about the animals we have studied."

Learning Activities Students will finish writing their sentences and paragraphs in the first 30 minutes.

For the last 15 minutes, gather the group and introduce Blabberize.com. Say, "Now that you have finished your paragraphs, I will show you a fun way of sharing your information. We will select a photo of your animal and 'Blabberize' it. Blabberize.com is a site that will take a picture and make it talk!" Show an example of a finished Blabber (http://youtu.be/i8egBSjPVAA). Next, show an instructional video about Blabberize.com (http://youtu.be/Vove1-R7Q9c).

Closure If time remains, ask students to exchange paragraphs.

Assessment Gather students' paragraphs and review them for completeness.

DAY SIX (45 minutes): Technology
Launching the Lesson: Activating Prior Knowledge
Review how to make a Blabber. First, demonstrate how to find the photos folder. Next, model how to create the mouth. Finally, read your paragraph to record the animal's voice. Remind students to practice their script aloud a few times before recording. If they do not like the results, they can re-record.

Learning Activities Students create their own Blabbers. Wander the room and help where needed. Students who finish first can help their classmates. It may take more than one day to complete the Blabbers, depending on the class.

Closure Say, "Thanks for all your hard work! Tomorrow, we'll have a film festival and watch each other's videos!"

Assessment Observe and mini-conference as students work. Check their products overnight for completeness.

DAY SEVEN (45 minutes): Film Festival
Launching the Lesson: Activating Prior Knowledge
Say, "Congratulations, Blabberizers! Today, we'll have a film festival and watch everyone's projects. As you watch, write down something you learned about each animal."

Learning Activities Play the videos while students note something about each one. At the end, ask them to share.

Closure Tell students, "These are some wonderful videos. You have taught each other so much. Can you think of other ways you might use Blabberize to teach something?"

Assessment Successful projects will have an introduction, closing, and at least three facts. The Blabber's mouth should move, and the student should speak clearly and fluently.

Extensions For deeper research on their animals, try exploring primary-friendly Web sites. See http://bit.ly/tsunami-links for suggestions.

WHAT CAN FIRST GRADERS DO TO KEEP OUR WORLD CLEAN AND BEAUTIFUL?

Keywords: environmental science, recycling, sequencing, how-to books

Ann O'Keefe

Always eager to be helpful, first graders are naturally enthusiastic to tackle challenges. This how-to lesson moves sequencing from an abstract idea to a concrete connection with the world around them. They're thrilled to discover that even if they are "just kids," the things they do actually make a difference. This lesson allows you to guide them from published informational texts through a synthesis process that leads to a book of their very own, and you can add in some time-telling practice, too!

Key Standard

Writing 1.7—Participate in shared research and writing projects (e.g., explore a number of how-to books on a given topic and use them to write a sequence of instructions).

To achieve this standard, students will need to be able to

- use words and phrases acquired through conversations, reading and being read to, and responding to texts, including using frequently occurring conjunctions to signal simple relationships, e.g., "because" (Language 1.6);
- identify the main topic and retell key details of a text (Reading Informational Text 1.2);
- identify basic similarities in and differences between two texts on the same topic, e.g., in illustrations, descriptions, or procedures (Reading Informational Text 1.9);
- participate in collaborative conversations with diverse partners about grade 1 topics and texts, with peers and adults in small and larger groups (Speaking and Listening 1.1);
- add drawings or other visual displays to descriptions when appropriate to clarify ideas, thoughts, and feelings (Speaking and Listening 1.5);
- with guidance and support from adults, recall information from experiences or gather information from provided sources to answer a question (Writing 1.8); and
- tell and write time in hours and half hours (Measurement and Data 1.3).

Time Needed

Stories and fact gathering can take place over one to three days; learning activities would take three 30- to 45-minute sessions.

Resource List

☑ An assortment of informational and/or picture books that focus on environmental, Earth Day, or recycling issues, such as:
- *10 Things I Can Do to Help My World: Fun and Easy Eco-tips* by Melanie Walsh (Candlewick Press, 2008)
- *Recycle! A Handbook for Kids* by Gail Gibbons (Little, Brown, 1992)
- *Recycling* by Rhonda Lucas Donald (Children's Press, 2002)
- *The Earth Book* by Todd Parr (New York: Little, Brown, 2010)
- *We Are Extremely Very Good Recyclers* by Lauren Child (Dial Books, 2009)
- *Kids Can Recycle* by Cecilia Minden (Cherry Lake, 2011)

☑ Chart paper

☑ Paper and writing supplies for making books

DAY ONE (45 minutes): Reading
Launching the Lesson: Activating Prior Knowledge

1. When your first graders gather for a story time or class meeting, point out the recycling bin in your room.
2. Ask, "Why do we have a recycling bin in our classroom?" Listen to answers, which will likely include the idea of saving trees since paper comes from trees. See how full your classroom bin is and wonder how many trees you're saving just with this one bin. "Does this help keep the world beautiful? Yes! So let's explore other ways we can help our world by reading some fiction and nonfiction books this week."
3. Tell the students, "While we do this research, let's keep a chart of all of the tips we learn. We get to start with one idea already: put used paper in a recycling bin!"
4. Read aloud a book or two about environmentalism, and as you go along, encourage the children to raise their hands when they see an idea for keeping the earth clean and beautiful. Add these to the chart.
5. You can use just one story time and two books for a brief lesson, or more than one day and several books if you have the time and materials. (Check with your school library. They often have several books on this topic!) Add to the chart whenever the kids notice a new tip, or add check marks to an already listed tip if it's in more than one book.

Learning Activities

1. When your chart has a substantial list of things that deal with environmental issues (turn out lights, shut off water, reduce, reuse, recycle, walk or ride bikes instead of using the car, compost, etc.), have the children sit in groups of four or five.
2. Give each group one large piece of paper to share so they can collaborate on and discuss the following. Say, "Of all the things on our research chart, try to list FIVE things that you can do easily and every day. There may be more than five things, but find your group's five favorite, best things."
3. Model a collaborative discussion for them using some of these guidelines:

   - Make sure everyone in your group gets to talk.
   - Take turns writing on the list after you've all agreed on a tip.
   - Use kind words such as, "That's a good idea, but do you think this one might be a little better?" or "I like this other idea, but let's choose yours this time."
   - Encourage them to ask questions of each other: "Why do you like that point so much?"

Closure and Observational Assessment
When you see that groups are finished, collect their lists. Briefly discuss how they are alike or different. If time is tight, say that you'll consult all of their good work and come up with a list for the whole class.

DAY TWO (40 minutes): Discussion
Launching the Lesson: Activating Prior Knowledge

1. Display the books you have used as read-alouds so that all of their covers are visible to the students. Conduct a discussion: Are some of them fiction? Did we learn facts from them anyway? Which ones are nonfiction or informational? Which book taught you the most? If you could buy one of these, which one would it be? Have them share their thoughts with a partner. Encourage them to give answers with evidence. Asking them to include the word *because* is an easy way to get students thinking in terms of evidence. For example,

   "I learned the most from that book *because* it had interesting pictures and a good list at the end."

2. Now share a list of five things you've culled from the students' group discussions. Write each tip on a sentence strip. Put them up on a board in any order. Then say, "Hey wait, I bet we can put these in chronological order with things we can do in the morning, during the day, and at night. Who can help me with that? Which one of these could you be sure to do every morning?" Guide them so that your list ends up looking something like this:

- Turn off water when I don't need it (morning, brushing teeth).
- Use both sides of paper (during school).
- Recycle and compost (at lunchtime).
- Ride my bike and walk more (after school).
- Turn off lights that I don't need (evening, bedtime).

3. Next, add time-telling concepts to this list. Let the kids help you assign real times of day to the list. Perhaps the first action would be at 8:00 a.m., the second at 10:30 a.m., etc.

Closure Tell the children that this is a great list containing wonderful thoughts they should share with kindergartners and other kids at your school. Tell them that next, they can each make their own book about caring for our world!

Assessment Be aware, during discussion, of misconceptions.

DAY THREE (45 minutes): Writing
Launching the Lesson: Activating Prior Knowledge
Say, "Last time, we listed things we could all do to help the earth, and we gave each event its own time."

Learning Activities
1. Today, students will synthesize their notes into a five-page book with a cover they design themselves (see page 25 for a template). It includes a blank clock face so students can be challenged to draw in the clock hands. There is room for both words and illustrations so that every child can express information at his or her level.
2. Your set should also include the sentence-starting words "first," "next," "then," and "finally," important words for sequential how-to writing. (See *How to Write a How-To* by Cecilia Minden and Kate Roth for in-depth help with leading students through the how-to process.)

Closure Collect the children's books and share them in class.

Assessment Observe the children during discussion and group work for active participation, oral expression, and cooperation. The final writing project will vary: some children will express themselves in complete sentences with punctuation, while others will rely on key words and pictures. Check for understanding of sequencing (did they keep the list in order?) and time telling (were they able to fill in the clocks accurately?).

Extensions Share the class books with the kindergarten classrooms for a couple of days. Alternatively, share them with your reading buddies or put them on display for an Earth Week celebration. To deepen the learning for gifted students, ask them to break down each task into its individual procedural steps. Students may also enjoy the online game I Don't Want to Clean My Room! (http://bit.ly/zpXqRN). Read the introductory comic strip together. Then they can play the game individually.

Name _____

___:00

First, _____

_____

_____

_____

_____

_____

From Navigating the Information Tsunami: Engaging Research Projects That Meet the Common Core State Standards, K-5. Cherry Lake Publishing, 2013.

HOW DO WE PLAN OUR ACTIVITIES AND CLOTHING FOR EACH SEASON?

Keywords: seasons, weather, opinions with evidence, Photo Story, audio recordings, slide shows
Andy Plemmons

First graders are naturally inquisitive learners eager to explore their world. In this lesson, students use print and/or digital resources to explore the four seasons. Students will create art and writing that demonstrates how they dress in their favorite season. The art and writing will combine into a final product using Photo Story (or PowerPoint), which can be shared with an audience.

Key Standard

Writing 1.8—With guidance and support from adults, recall information from experiences or gather information from provided sources to answer a question.

To accomplish this standard, students will need to be able to

- ask and answer questions about key details in a text (Reading Informational Text 1.1);
- know and use various text features (e.g., headings, tables of contents, glossaries, electronic menus, icons) to locate key facts or information in a text (Reading Informational Text 1.5);
- use the illustrations and details in a text to describe its key idea (Reading Informational Text 1.7);
- add drawings or other visual displays to descriptions when appropriate to clarify ideas, thoughts, and feelings (Speaking and Listening 1.5); and
- produce complete sentences when appropriate to the task and situation (Speaking and Listening 1.6).

Time Needed

Five 45- to 60-minute sessions

Resource List

- ☑ Items of clothing representing the seasons (e.g., rain boots, scarf, mittens, shorts, sandals, etc.)
- ☑ Index cards
- ☑ Note-taking chart (see page 27)
- ☑ Script sheet (see page 30)
- ☑ Document camera
- ☑ Pencils, crayons, and/or markers
- ☑ Paper doll template (http://bit.ly/xaEUY7)
- ☑ Construction paper
- ☑ PebbleGo Earth and Space database (subscription, http://pebblego.com) or the Exploring the Seasons series by Terri DeGezelle (Capstone/Pebble Plus, 2012)
- ☑ Digital cameras
- ☑ Computer with Photo Story 3 for Windows or PowerPoint installed
- ☑ Computer headsets or microphones

DAY ONE (45–60 minutes): Learning About Seasons
Launching the Lesson: Activating Prior Knowledge

1. Invite first graders to sit on the floor with a partner. Say, "Today, we're going to start exploring the four seasons. I'm going to hold up some items. Think about what the weather might be like outside when you wear or use these items. First, think to yourself, and then turn to your partner and share."
2. Hold up objects until each has been shown and students have talked with a partner.
3. Say, "Now that you've talked about these items, let's see if we can sort our objects in different ways. What was one of the kinds of weather that you described to your partner?" A response might be "raining" or "hot." "Raining is a great place to start. Here's an index card with the word raining on it. What were the items that we might wear or use if it's raining?"

4. Invite students to begin sorting items into groups on the floor and naming the groups with index cards. Say, "Now that we're starting to think about weather and how it impacts what we use and wear, it's time for us to consider some questions. Over the next few days, we'll explore these questions in books and on the computer. We'll also write, draw, and record what we discover. We'll ask ourselves, What is the weather in fall, winter, spring, and summer? What kinds of things do we do in fall, winter, spring, and summer? What do we wear outside in fall, winter, spring, and summer?"

Learning Activities

1. Say, "Now we're going to the computers. A database called PebbleGo will be on your screen. Click on each season, listen to the text, and watch the videos. As you watch and listen, write down facts or draw pictures to show what you've learned about our three questions. Our librarian will be working with us today to use PebbleGo and find answers to our questions. As you finish looking for information on the computer, move back to the tables and look through the seasons books. If you have trouble reading the words, use the pictures in the books to help you learn about activities and clothing in the four seasons."

2. Students click through the Web pages for each season, making notes on the chart shown below. The adults support students as they search.

Name:

Fall (What's the weather? What activities do people do? What should you wear?)	**Winter** (What's the weather? What activities do people do? What should you wear?)
Spring (What's the weather? What activities do people do? What should you wear?)	**Summer** (What's the weather? What activities do people do? What should you wear?)

From Navigating the Information Tsunami: Engaging Research Projects That Meet the Common Core State Standards, K-5. Cherry Lake Publishing, 2013.

Closure Say, "Thank you, everyone, for your great work today. Please hand me your paper as you line up. Tomorrow, we'll write out what we have learned."

Assessment Collect student papers and reflect on their work. Note the students with whom you should mini-conference to correct misconceptions.

DAY TWO (45–60 minutes): Scriptwriting
Launching the Lesson: Activating Prior Knowledge

1. Select a few positive examples of the Day One graphic organizer. Use a document camera to display them as you read them aloud.
2. Say, "Look at all that we discovered yesterday on the computers and in books. Those resources really helped us answer our three questions. Now that we know this information, we should think about our own lives in each of these seasons. What things do you like to do in each of the seasons? Now that you know what the weather is like in each of the seasons, what would you wear outside? Let's take some time today to write about your favorite of the four seasons. I have an organizer that has beginnings of sentences to get you started. While you write, use your organizer from yesterday to help you. I'll come around to conference with you."
3. Students complete the script sheet on page 30. Students who did not finish their research from Day One could work with another adult, such as the school librarian, before moving to the sentence portion of this project. If students need additional time, this portion of the lesson could be extended into another writing workshop time. Students who finish early can begin the next day's activity. (Having students working at different rates will actually make the recording process later on easier!)

Closure Say, "As our writing time comes to an end today, let's share our sentences with a partner. As you listen to your partner's work, check to see if you agree that the weather, activities, and clothing match what you know about each season. If you don't agree, tell your partner why and show what you found in your research."

DAY THREE (45–60 minutes): Art

1. This session can be done in the classroom or in collaboration with the art teacher. If done in art, more time can be spent on collecting research or writing sentences.
2. Say, "Now that we have an understanding of each season's weather, activities, and clothing, let's think about how we can make that visual. Today, you will have a chance to create art of your favorite season. Draw a scene that matches the weather and draw clothes on your paper doll that you would wear during that season. I have paper, paper doll cutouts, and coloring supplies for you to use. Remember to think about the research that we did."
3. Students may refer to their script sheet (on page 30) while they complete their art. Talk with students about their drawings to check for understanding of the weather and seasons. If confusion occurs, refer students back to their research resources, the librarian, or a partner to clarify their misconceptions. Confirm that students' names are on the front of the scene and the back of their paper doll. As a digital alternative, have students draw in Kid Pix and export each drawing as an image.

DAY FOUR (45–60 minutes): Photography

1. Days Four and Five need additional adult support (e.g., the librarian, parent or community volunteers, or an instructional coach). If computer equipment or adult support is limited, set up this activity as a center and ask students to cycle through.

2. Say, "I am so excited by the work that you all have accomplished. Based on your research, you each have sentences, a scene, and a paper doll that show what you have learned about your favorite season. We'll be putting your pictures together into a slide show with your voice. Today, our goal is to take pictures of our paper dolls in the scene and save those pictures on the computer."

3. In the classroom or library, students assemble their paper doll in the scene. Using a digital camera, and with guidance from an adult, they photograph their scene. An adult will help import the photos to the computer, add them into Photo Story 3 (or PowerPoint or preferred slide/presentation software), and sequence them.

DAY FIVE (45–60 minutes): Record Narration

1. Have the computer headset or microphone plugged in and the slide show loaded.

2. Say, "Yesterday, you each took photographs of your scenes and paper dolls. Today, while you are in writer's workshop, you will take turns using a program called Photo Story 3 (or PowerPoint's Record Narration feature, which allows a new audio file to be recorded on each slide) to record the sentences you wrote a few days ago. It is important for you to make sure that you record the correct sentences on the correct photograph, so check yourself as you go. The librarian will call you up when it is your turn and help you make your recording. When you each finish, we will have a class movie of everyone's projects that we can watch in class or show other people."

3. One at a time, students will use their scripts to record their voice on their slide. Adult assistance will help monitor for accuracy, guide them in recording, and save frequently. When each student has recorded, allow the student to listen and check his or her work.

Closure Say, "Great job today, everybody! Now, let's view our projects as a class. As you listen, think about whether or not you agree with what you hear. Use the research you have done to help you decide."

Assessment As adults have checked for understanding at each phase of the process, no formal assessment is necessary. A successful final product will answer the questions about what the weather is, what activities can be done, and what to wear in each of the four seasons.

Extensions Students can host a viewing of their final products by parents, community members, or other classes. As guests view the final products, students can explain their learning process. Additionally, students can investigate what causes weather to change. Record and graph weather at home and ask out-of-town relatives or friends to share the weather where they are. Watch the news or learn to read a weather forecast online.

My Favorite Season

by _____

My favorite season is _____ because _____

_____

_____

_____ .

Outside, I like to _____ . I wear _____

_____

_____

_____ .

I never wear _____ because then I would be too

_____

_____ !

From Navigating the Information Tsunami: Engaging Research Projects That Meet the Common Core State Standards, K-5. Cherry Lake Publishing, 2013.

Grade 2

WHAT PRESIDENT SHOULD WE ADD TO MOUNT RUSHMORE?

Keywords: national parks, presidents, biography, persuasive writing, American history

Suzy Rabbat and Sara Wilkie

Second graders are eager to learn about the world beyond their neighborhood. In this lesson, students conduct biographical research in order to weigh in on which U.S. president should be added to Mount Rushmore.

Key Standard

Writing 2.1—Write opinion pieces in which they introduce the topic or book they are writing about, state an opinion, supply reasons that support the opinion, use linking words (e.g., because, and, also) to connect opinion and reasons, and provide a concluding statement or section.

To accomplish this standard, students will need to be able to

- navigate Web content;
- draw conclusions from informational text;
- use conventions effectively; and
- weigh evidence against a set of criteria.

Time Needed

Three 40- to 45-minute sessions

Resource List

☑ *Visit Mount Rushmore* by Mary O'Mara (Gareth Stevens, 2012)

☑ Facts4Me.com online subscription database

☑ Chart paper and markers

☑ A class wiki (see http://bit.ly/wikispaces-teachers) with a template formatted according to page 33 (for instructions, see http://bit.ly/wikispaces-template)

Optional Resources

☑ Age- and grade-appropriate informational texts about the presidents

☑ *What Does the President Do?* by Amanda Miller (Children's Press, 2009)

☑ *Who Carved the Mountain? The Story of Mount Rushmore* by Jean L. S. Patrick (Mount Rushmore History Association, 2005)

DAY ONE (45 minutes): Introduction
Launching the Lesson: Activating Prior Knowledge

1. Ask, "Has anyone visited Mount Rushmore? Tell us what you saw there." Encourage students to share their experience. Then say, "Let's read to find out more about Mount Rushmore."
2. Read *Visit Mount Rushmore* by Mary O'Mara aloud to the class. In addition to providing interesting historical information, this book also talks about the rationale for selecting Washington, Jefferson, Lincoln, and Roosevelt.

Learning Activities

1. Take time to discuss the information in the read-aloud that provides rationale for selecting the presidents. Write the heading, "Qualities of an Outstanding President" on the chart paper. Ask, "Do you remember why those four presidents were chosen for Mount Rushmore?" Add their responses to the chart. "Washington was our first president. He set a good example for others." Write "sets a good example for others" on the chart. Lincoln helped put an end to slavery. Say, "So by doing that, he made life better for many people." Write, "improved the lives of others" on the chart. Continue the same with Jefferson and Roosevelt. Then explain the essential question.

2. Say, "Geologists recently discovered there is enough space on Mount Rushmore to carve the head of one more president. You have been commissioned, or given the job, to select the next president to be carved on Mount Rushmore! Which president should we honor? How will we decide? We know why the original four presidents were chosen."

3. Refer to the chart. "Are there any other qualities we should think about in selecting a president for this honor?" This topic can also be linked to character education, especially the concept of leadership.

4. To help students zero in on leadership qualities, ask them to name some people they see as leaders. Responses may include their principal, Cub Scout leader, or the mayor of their town. Then ask, "What makes a good leader?" Add their suggestions to the list of qualities. Keep your list of qualities/accomplishments to four or five broad ideas—e.g., fair, well liked, improved our country. Students will use this as their criteria for selecting a president.

5. Then say, "The work on Mount Rushmore began in 1927. At that time, Calvin Coolidge was our country's president. He was the 30th president of the United States. Out of 30 presidents, only four were chosen for this monument. Your task is a little bigger! Barack Obama is our 44th president. Let's do the math. We already have four presidents on Mount Rushmore. That leaves...right! There are 40 presidents left, and your job is to select one of those 40! How will we go about this? We need a plan."

6. With a computer connected to an LCD projector, navigate to the database Facts4Me. com. Click on the link to the presidents. They are listed in chronological order by term of office. "Since George Washington was our first president and he's already on Mount Rushmore, we'll start with our second president, John Adams." Model how to navigate to the information about John Adams. "Let's take another look at our leadership qualities." Ask students to read them aloud.

7. Continue by saying, "Now let's look at what is written about John Adams. Some of the information tells about his family and his hobbies. This information is 'nice to know.' Some of the information may give us clues about his leadership qualities. This information is what we 'need to know.' We'll read the first paragraph, then stop and see if what we read was nice to know or if it's what we need to know."

8. Give the students time to read the first paragraph silently. "Now, put one hand behind your back. I'll say 'think, decide, ready, show!' Think about what you read, decide if the information was nice to know or need to know. Does it help us understand if John Adams was a good leader? 'Ready' means position your thumb: thumbs-up if this is something you need to know, thumbs-down if it's nice to know. When I say 'show,' bring your hand out in front of you and share your answer. Let's practice. The first paragraph talks about John Adams, his wife, and three sons. Think (put your hands behind your back!): Is this nice to know or need to know? Decide, does this information connect to our qualities? Ready, put your thumb up for yes or thumb down for no. Be sure to get your thumb ready while it's behind your back. Show! Bring your hand out in front of you." The purpose of this strategy is to engage everyone in processing the information. Say, "Wonderful! Can someone tell me why you had your thumb down?" Students should explain that information about his family doesn't show what kind of leader he was.

9. Then say, "Let's go on to the next paragraph. This one begins with the statement, 'President Adams was not popular. He was stuck-up and stubborn. He had lots of enemies.' Think, decide, ready, show." Hopefully thumbs will be pointing up. Students should determine this is "need to know" information that addresses John Adams's character. Say, "This sentence is a clue about his character. It gives us evidence to say that John Adams was not well liked. We would not recommend him for Mount Rushmore. Let's record that evidence on the wiki."

10. Bring up the wiki template (shown below or at http://bit.ly/tsunami-links) on the large screen and show students how to edit, record their information, and save. Ask students to answer each question with yes, no, or sometimes, then add "because" and the reason why. Continue reading the entry on John Adams to determine if there is additional evidence to support the decision to eliminate him in our search for a president.

Qualities of an Outstanding President—Wiki Template

President	Did he set a good example for others?	Well liked?	Improved the lives of others?	Fair?	Improved our country?
John Adams		No, because he was • stubborn • had lots of enemies			
Eisenhower		Yes, because everyone wore *I like Ike* buttons.	Yes, because he ended the war in Korea.	Yes, because he protected black children who wanted to go to school with white children.	Yes, because he built highways to make it easier for people to travel.
Kennedy			Yes, because he helped the poor by starting the Peace Corps.		
Johnson				Yes, because he wanted the United States to be a place where anyone could get an education.	

Closure Say, "Today we learned about Mount Rushmore and discovered that we have been commissioned with the important job of deciding which president to add to this monument. We also practiced reading like a detective, looking for clues or evidence to help us make a decision. Tomorrow you will practice your detective skills as you read about other presidents."

Assessment Give students the following exit slip. Students may refer to the qualities listed on the chart or an example from the modeled text.

Name _____

Think about your task to find the next president for Mount Rushmore. As you read about a president:

What kind of information is nice to know? Explain or give an example. _____

_____

_____

What kind of information is nice to know? Explain or give an example. _____

_____

_____

_____

What kind of information do you need to know to help you decide on a president? Explain or give an example. _____

_____

_____

_____

From Navigating the Information Tsunami: Engaging Research Projects That Meet the Common Core State Standards, K-5. Cherry Lake Publishing, 2013.

DAY TWO (45 minutes): Research
Launching the Lesson: Activating Prior Knowledge

1. Having modeled the note-taking process in the previous lesson, students will work with a partner to continue the presidential research. Define the roles of reader and recorder. Say, "The reader will read the information out loud. The recorder will type the evidence in the wiki template. Remember, both reader and recorder are thinkers! Be sure to talk about your evidence and decision before you add information to the wiki. When you finish with one president, switch jobs before you begin researching the next president. We will do our research in the library where the librarian will show us how to find Facts4Me and our class wiki. The librarian and I will be available to help you as you look for evidence to make a decision on the presidents assigned to you."

2. Depending on the time you have to devote to this research, you may decide to pare the original list of 40 presidents down to a smaller number, perhaps focusing on more contemporary presidents. Consider assigning the same president to more than one group. For example, Group A may research Presidents Eisenhower, Kennedy, and Johnson; and Group B might research Kennedy, Johnson, and Nixon. This would give students the opportunity to collaborate with other groups to confirm their decisions and verify their evidence, or it may challenge them to take a second look at their information source.

Learning Activities

1. Arrange students so they are sitting side by side—ideally, each with his or her own computer. The reader can navigate to the Presidents page on Facts4Me.com, and the recorder will navigate to the wiki page. Be sure to display the chart paper of criteria where all can see.

2. As students read and discuss the text, they will record their claim on their wiki page using this sentence format:

> yes/no/sometimes + because + evidence
> *Example: Yes, because he was a military leader during World War II.*

3. Once they have completed their research, encourage them to view the claims and evidence posted by other groups who researched the same president. Do they agree? Do they need to go back and confirm their evidence? Should they verify their information in another source, like an informational text or encyclopedia?

4. Ask the librarian to display a large chart with the names of the presidents in the library. Next to each name, make two columns. Label one "Yes" and the other "No." As students complete their research, have them place a sticker dot on the column to show their recommendation. This will also show where there are discrepancies in opinion.

Closure Allow time at the end of the lesson for students to comment on each other's wiki page using the Discussion tab. To ensure that everyone receives a comment, direct students to view and comment on the group that appears below their team. The last team on the list can comment on the first team's page. They might compliment the team for their strong evidence or be curious to learn more about the presidents that a group is researching.

Assessment Reading each group's wiki page will give you an indication of whether or not students were able to extract relevant information to support their claim with evidence from the text. If time allows, you may wish to extend the research activity for one more day, providing time for students to search in additional resources to gather more evidence. Ask the librarian to help locate age- and grade-appropriate informational texts and/or online resources to supplement the research.

DAY THREE (40 minutes): Writing
Launching the Lesson: Activating Prior Knowledge

Say, "By now each team has identified at least one president they would recommend and one they would not recommend. Your job is to share your opinion in writing. You can write about a president that deserves this honor, or write about one you feel does not deserve to be on Mount Rushmore. It is your choice. Have you ever helped someone cook something that was wonderfully delicious? Many people follow a recipe when they cook. As you write about your president, you'll be following a writing recipe. Let's take a look."

Learning Activities

1. Say, "A recipe has a list of ingredients. What happens when we leave out an ingredient? What if I were making a veggie omelet and forgot to include the eggs?" Students will respond that you'll just have vegetables, but not an omelet.

2. Say, "That's right. What if I bake oatmeal cookies and leave out the sugar?" (They would not be sweet.) "So a recipe helps us remember all the ingredients to include in our cooking and baking to make sure it comes out right. In the same way, we are going to follow a writing recipe as we write about a president we've researched. The recipe will help us think about all the important pieces to include in our writing."

3. Show the figures below. Say, "Here are the ingredients for our writing recipe."

Closure Students can share their opinion pieces by reading them to the class or making them accessible for others to read. One effective way to do this is to share them on a class Web site, wiki, or blog. This opens up the audience to include family, friends, and students from other schools. Consider narrowing down the choices by having students vote. Before casting their vote, ask students to write the reason for their selection on the ballot. Requiring students to share their rationale gives them another opportunity to state a claim and provide evidence. After several primary elections, you may find a winner for Mount Rushmore!

1. FIRST, TELL ABOUT MOUNT RUSHMORE
Why is it special? Is there something you can share about its history? Explain your task to find a fifth president.

2. SECOND, GIVE YOUR OPINION
Who do you think the fifth president should be, or who do you think should not be chosen?

3. THIRD, GIVE REASONS THAT SUPPORT YOUR OPINION
Include the evidence you found in your research. Use linking words (because, and, also) to show how your opinion and evidence go together. Here is an example: I don't think John Adams would be a good choice to add to Mount Rushmore because he was not well liked by the people. He was stubborn and stuck-up.

4. LAST, YOUR WRITING NEEDS A FINAL TOUCH LIKE ADDING THE FROSTING ON THE CAKE
For your final touch, write a final sentence that tells your opinion one more time: Because John Adams was not a good leader, I think he should not be added to Mount Rushmore.

Assessment This project is formatively assessed at each step of the project. Ask students to self-assess at the project's conclusion.

Self-Assessment

My project is written to persuade.	Yes	No
I started by talking about Mount Rushmore's history.	Yes	No
I focused my essay on one president to add or not add.	Yes	No
I had at least three reasons.	Yes	No
I explained each reason.	Yes	No
I ended with a concluding sentence.	Yes	No
I presented my project to the class.	Yes	No
I worked well with my partner.	Yes	No

From Navigating the Information Tsunami: Engaging Research Projects That Meet the Common Core State Standards, K-5. Cherry Lake Publishing, 2013.

Extensions To provide an authentic audience, consider sharing student work with author Jean L. S. Patrick (jean@jeanpatrick.com), who has extensively researched and written two books for children about Mount Rushmore. Second graders will also enjoy reading her Mount Rushmore FAQs posted on her Web site (www.jeanpatrick.com/mount_rushmore_FAQS.htm).

Acknowledgement: Much appreciation to Leon Braisted for sharing his student debate topic: Which American President should be added to those portrayed on Mt. Rushmore?

TSUNAMI TIP: Let Your Computer Read Aloud to You!

In second grade, the distance between strong and weaker readers in your class may become more pronounced. To help bridge the gap, try your computer's read-aloud feature.

If you have a Mac, go to the Apple Icon, then System Preferences, and then Speech. Click on Text to Speech. Click "Speak selected text when the key is pressed," then click the Select key. Ann O'Keefe (see page 22) set hers to Control+Option+Command+S. Once this is set up, students can highlight text in any application, press the four keys simultaneously, and the highlighted text will be read aloud.

If you have a PC, try a free download of Naturalreader.com, which works similarly (also available for Mac).

IF ROCKS COULD TALK, WHAT STORIES WOULD THEY TELL US ABOUT THE PAST?

Keywords: rocks, minerals, learning with objects, informational writing

Suzy Rabbat and Sara Wilkie

Second graders are curious and eager to learn. As evolving readers, they are continuously expanding their basic literacy skills and building their vocabulary. They show their understanding of informational text by summarizing what they've read, answering how and why questions, comparing information from various sources, and connecting information and ideas to their own life experiences.

Key Standard

Writing 2.7—Participate in shared research and writing projects (e.g., read a number of books on a single topic to produce a report; record science observations).

To accomplish this standard, students will need to be able to
- formulate questions;
- use a table of contents or index to locate information;
- locate and use information on an age-appropriate electronic resource; and
- record notes on paper or on a wiki using a template.

Time Needed
- Three 45-minute sessions

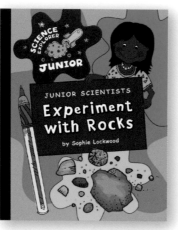

Resource List
☑ Chart paper divided into two columns, labeled "Know" and "Wonder"
☑ Markers for chart paper
☑ Various types of rocks, or photos of different rocks mounted on index cards
☑ Chart paper divided into four columns, titled "Properties of Rocks"
☑ Introductory text: *Rock* by Chris Oxlade (Heinemann, 2002)
☑ Informational texts about sedimentary, igneous, and metamorphic rocks.
☑ Suggested titles include:
- *Rock Records* by Beth Geiger (National Geographic, 2006)
- *Rock Formations* by Connor Dayton (PowerKids Press, 2007)
- *Rocks and Fossils* by William McConnell (Rosen, 2003)
- *Rocks and Minerals* by Dana Meachen Rau (Cherry Lake, 2009), for advanced readers
- Facts4Me.com (subscription); or Rock Hounds—Rock Creations, free from the Franklin Institute (www.fi.edu/fellows/fellow1/oct98/create/index.html)
☑ Computers with drawing software (e.g., Kid Pix, Microsoft Paint, TuxPaint) or paper, pencil, and crayons/markers for writing activity

DAY ONE (45 minutes): Learning About Rocks
Launching the Lesson: Activating Prior Knowledge

1. Invite second graders to sit in a circle on the floor.
2. Place a group of objects in the middle of the circle and ask students to sort them into two categories: rocks and non-rocks. Begin by asking, "Is there an item you can identify as a rock or non-rock? Who would like to begin the sort?" Have a student select an object from the center of the circle and declare it rock or non-rock. Move the item to a new place in the circle and continue until you have two distinct groups.

Note: In addition to the rocks, include other hard items like a wooden spoon, plastic pencil holder, or something made of steel. Also consider rocks that may have been carved into shapes. As you discuss the properties of rocks, students will have to go beyond using hardness as a criterion for rocks.

3. Then ask, "How did you determine which items were rocks?" Record their responses under the "Know" column of the chart.

Learning Activities

1. Say, "Rocks are a natural material. They are made of minerals. Some rocks are a mixture of minerals; others are made of one mineral like silver or gold. All rocks do not look the same because they are formed in different ways and made of different minerals. Minerals are also found in nature, but they are not living things. For example, salt is a mineral."

2. Say, "We can describe rocks by naming their properties. A property is a trait that tells you something about an object. Color is a property." Title a large chart paper "Properties of Rocks." Divide the paper into four columns. Label the first column "Color." Ask students to name the colors they see in the rocks that were sorted. Record their responses on the chart.

3. Say, "What are some other properties or traits to describe these rocks?" Someone may answer smooth or bumpy. "These words describe how the rock feels. We can call that trait texture." Label the next column "Texture." Add "smooth" and "bumpy" in this column. Then ask, "Are there other texture words we can add to the list (e.g., rough, scratchy)?" Continue generating adjectives to describe the properties of rocks. Elicit responses to address the properties of luster (e.g., shiny, dull, metallic) and hardness. Label the last two columns "Luster" and "Hardness." Post the chart in a place where it is visible to all so that students can use it as a word bank when they begin to write about rocks in Lesson 3.

   Before continuing, clear up any misconceptions (e.g., non-rock items that some students identified as rocks).

4. Read aloud *Rock* by Chris Oxlade or another informational text about rocks to build background knowledge and spark students' interest. Oxlade's book talks about properties of rocks and introduces various ways rocks are made, without categorizing them into sedimentary, igneous, and metamorphic.

5. Focus students' attention on the Know-Wonder chart. Then say, "We made several observations about the properties of rocks. We also listened to a book about rocks. Is there anything that we learned from this book's expert author that we want to change or add to our Know column? Take a few minutes to think about questions you have about rocks." Pause for a minute or two.

6. Then say, "Turn to an 'Elbow Buddy.' This is someone who is sitting near you, someone you can touch elbows with. Share your questions with your Elbow Buddy." Providing a little thinking time, along with the opportunity to share with one classmate, draws all students into the wonder component of inquiry.

7. Supply students with large sticky notes. Say, "Write your questions on the sticky notes. If you have more than one question, use a new sticky note for each question. Then place your questions on the chart in the Wonder column."

Closure Share the questions in the Wonder column: either read them aloud or ask the students to read their questions to the class.

Formative Assessment Review students' questions posted on the Know-Wonder chart. Is there any confusion or misunderstanding about the definition of a rock?

DAY TWO (45 minutes): Research
Launching the Lesson: Activating Prior Knowledge

1. Set up five to six stations on desks in the classroom or tables in the library. Place three rocks in each station. Include one of each type: sedimentary, igneous, and metamorphic. Label the rocks with numbers. For ease of discussion, use the same three types of rocks at each station. Another option is to use photos of the same three rocks.

2. Revisit the questions generated on the Know-Wonder chart (page 39) and focus on the ones that can be answered by knowing how rocks are formed. Say to students, "In order to understand why rocks look and feel different, we will need to understand how rocks are made. Geologists are people who study rocks and soil. They have grouped rocks into three categories. These categories are sedimentary, igneous, and metamorphic. Today, you will become an 'expert' on one of those categories. Your job is to find out how one kind of rock is made. We'll use a database called Facts4Me on the computers in the library. Our librarian will show us how to use Facts4Me to find the information we need."

Learning Activities

1. Assign students to one of three groups: igneous, sedimentary, or metamorphic. The librarian can demonstrate how to navigate to the information related to their rock type at Facts4Me.com—just two clicks away. Click on Rocks and Minerals, then select Igneous Rock, Metamorphic Rock, or Sedimentary Rock.

2. Using the Rock Detective Guide (page 42), say, "Today you will be a rock detective. As you read the information on Facts4Me.com, look for clues in the text to help you understand how your type of rock is formed. Write those clues on your Rock Detective Guide. Next, look for words that describe the properties of your rock." (Refer to the chart generated on Day One to remind students what is meant by *properties*.)

3. Say, "Record those words on your Rock Detective Guide as well. Finally, tell about something we may see or use that is made of this type of rock. Don't forget to study the photos and captions as you read. You may find some important clues there. When you have gathered all your clues, bring your detective guide to the librarian or me. We have one more piece of detective work for you to complete before you solve this case." The information in Facts4Me is concise and appropriate for second-grade researchers. Circulate around the computers with your librarian, assisting students in locating the needed information. This step should take approximately 10 minutes.

4. Once students have gathered all their clues, do a quick scan for accuracy. Then, direct students to one of the stations. Say, "Now that you've gathered clues about sedimentary rocks on your Rock Detective Guide, take a close look at the three rocks at your station. Use your clues to determine which rock is an example of a sedimentary rock. Once you decide, write the number of the rock on the bottom of your guide. Add a sentence telling why you chose this rock. What were the clues that helped you decide? Compare your ideas with another sedimentary rock detective. Do you agree? If not, can you explain to this detective why your rock choice is different? Use the sentence on the bottom of your detective guide to explain your choice."

5. If students finish early, have rock samples, magnifying glasses, and rock field guides located in other areas of the room for children to explore until all detectives have completed their tasks. Consider including samples of unusual rocks like pumice (a rock that floats), sulfur (a rock with a strong odor), and fossils!

Closure and Formative Assessment

1. When everyone has identified their rock, invite the children to gather on the rug. Classroom teachers and librarians can partner on guiding students through the synthesis of their research. One can lead the following discussion while the other writes the students' findings on large chart paper or on a word-processing document projected on a large screen for all to see.

2. Say, "We are going to share what we've learned about the formation of rocks from each group's research. We'll start with the Sedimentary Rock Detectives. Let's ask that group to explain how sedimentary rocks are formed." Using their Rock Detective Guides, students in the sedimentary group will share what they've learned about the formation of sedimentary rocks. The group should include the concept of layers of rock built up and flattened over time.

3. Then say, "Sedimentary Detectives, please tell us about the properties of this type of rock." Students may provide words that describe the color, texture, luster, and/or hardness. (Pass around samples of sedimentary rock.) Finally, ask, "What story might this rock tell us about the past?" Possible answers may include: The rock might tell about storms that carried layers of mud, shells, and sand. Each layer is like a new chapter in the story. Some sedimentary rocks contain fossils. Those rocks could tell about the living thing that left a mark on the rock. Repeat with the Igneous and Metamorphic Rock Detectives.

DAY THREE (45 minutes): Writing
Launching the Lesson: Activating Prior Knowledge

1. Explain to the class that they will share what they've learned about rocks in a writing project. Each student will describe an igneous, sedimentary, or metaphoric rock. Provide two options.

2. Say, "You can choose which kind of rock to write about: the kind you researched and wrote about on the Rock Detective Guide, or one of the rock types you learned about from the other rock detectives using the information on the charts. This checklist (below) tells what to include in your writing."

3. Show students how to begin their writing, with a topic sentence such as:

☐ If my (sedimentary/igneous/metamorphic) rock could talk, it would tell you…
☐ My (sedimentary/igneous/metamorphic) rock knows a lot about the past.
☐ My (sedimentary/igneous/metamorphic) rock has been around for a very long time.
☐ It started…

4. Give students a copy of the Writing Checklist so they can track their progress.

Writing Checklist
☐ I begin with a topic sentence.
☐ I name the type of rock I am writing about.
☐ I use at least five words to describe the properties of my rock. (Use the word bank!)
☐ I tell how this rock was formed and what it might tell us about the past.
☐ I drew a picture or took a photo of my rock.

Rock Detective Guide

Detective's Name _____

Step 1: Gathering Clues

I am looking for clues about _____ rocks.

Here's how they are made.	This is what they look like.
Some examples are...	These are some ways people use them today.

Step 2: Using My Clues

I am using my eyes to make a close observation and using my clues to help me find a sedimentary rock. _____

_____

I think rock number _____ is an example of a sedimentary rock because _____

_____ .

From Navigating the Information Tsunami: Engaging Research Projects That Meet the Common Core State Standards, K-5. Cherry Lake Publishing, 2013.

5. Students can work independently or collaboratively with a partner to complete the writing assignment. The task can be done with paper and pencil, or students can compose their writing using a word-processing program. Illustrations can be hand drawn or created with a computer program like Kid Pix and inserted into their word-processing document. Alternatively, students may prefer to draw by hand, scan their drawing, and insert the image file into a typed document with Photo Story or PowerPoint, as described in the weather lesson on page 26, or one of the tools in the Dust Bowl unit beginning on page 79.

6. For an online publishing option, try Fotobabble.com, similar to Blabberize (see page 18). Scan the artwork and upload the image file to Fotobabble. Then have students record their writing in Fotobabble. Embed the completed files in the class wiki.

Extensions As an extension activity, encourage students to explore types of rock found around the world. Investigate the types of rocks that were used to build the Great Pyramids in Egypt, the Great Wall of China, Machu Picchu, the Taj Mahal, even the White House! For hands-on learning, check out the experiments in *Super Cool Science Experiments: Rocks* by Sophie Lockwood (Cherry Lake, 2010).

TSUNAMI TIP: ADJUSTING LESSONS TO FIT YOUR GRADE LEVEL

Many of the Common Core State Standards for one grade are similar to those of adjoining grades. Consider adapting lessons designed for the grade below or above that of your students. For example, contributor Andy Plemmons (page 26) studied rocks with kindergarteners instead of second graders. To see how his young learners engaged in learning about rocks, visit http://bit.ly/barrow-rocks.

Grade 3
HOW ARE ANIMALS CONNECTED VIA THE FOOD CHAIN? HOW DO HABITATS IMPACT ANIMALS?

Keywords: animals, habitats, biomes, food chain, food web, adventure stories, storyboarding, comics

Kara Fribley, Eileen Thomas, and Kristin Fontichiaro

Third graders are enthusiastic for work that is fun. This lesson combines two short research tasks (one as a group, one solo) before asking students to synthesize their understanding of animals, food chains, and habitats in an original animal adventure story. Consider pairing this project with a literature circle or class read-aloud from Avi's Poppy series. Partner-teach this lesson with your school librarian or other learning specialist.

Key Standards

Writing 3.4—With guidance and support from adults, produce writing in which development and organization are appropriate to the task and purpose.

Writing 3.5—With guidance and support from peers and adults, develop and strengthen writing as needed by planning, revising, and editing.

Writing 3.7—Conduct short research projects that build knowledge about a topic.

To accomplish these standards, students will need to be able to

- extract information and images from digital resources;
- scan documents or take digital photos;
- import digital images into a wiki page; and
- sequence a story.

Time Needed

Eight 30-60 minute sessions

Resource List

☑ Computers with Web access for sites listed at http://bit.ly/tsunami-links
☑ Class wiki (see pages 45 and 46 for guidance) or paper and pencil for note making
☑ *Who Eats What? Food Chains and Food Webs* by Patricia Lauber, illustrated by Holly Keller (Scholastic 1992, 2005)
☑ Chart paper and markers
☑ Print comics (or access to www.professorgarfield.org/toon_book_reader/)

DAY ONE (30 minutes): Introduction to Food Webs
Launching the Lesson: Activating Prior Knowledge

Show students the cover of *Who Eats What?* What does Keller's cover illustration show? What questions do students have? Record these on chart paper.

Learning Activities

Read the text aloud, pausing to model your thinking and questions aloud.

Closure Return to the chart paper. Which questions were answered by the text? What new things did they learn? Add those to the chart paper.

Assessment Observation of student discussion.

DAYS TWO AND THREE (60 minutes each): Biome Research
Launching the Lesson: Activating Prior Knowledge
Review Day One's chart paper.

Learning Activities
1. Discuss how animals in a food web must live near one another in order for the food chain or web to survive. Different areas of the world are divided into biomes, or habitats. Each biome has unique weather (e.g., dry, humid, hot, cold), land formations (e.g., flatlands, mountains), and bodies of water (e.g., ponds, rivers, lakes, oceans).
2. Remind students of the animal adventures they know (e.g., Avi's Poppy series or E. B. White's *Stuart Little* or *The Trumpet of the Swan*). Tell students that they will create an animal adventure as a comic! To do so, they will need to conduct a few phases of research.
3. Their first research will be done in a group. They will learn about the climate, animals, and plants of a specific biome.
4. Divide students into groups of four by biome. Blue Planet Biomes was created specifically for elementary learners and is recommended. Try tundra (or arctic), desert, grasslands, savanna, deciduous forest, and rain forest. For larger classes, add taiga or alpine. Chaparral is a good option for students who struggle with reading.
5. Give each group two computers: one for research and one for the wiki template (for a sample, see http://bit.ly/tsunami-links). Set up the template in advance with these questions to guide student research:

> 1. Who is in your group?
> 2. What is the name of your biome?
> 3. What is the weather like?
> 4. What is the land like?
> 5. What kinds of bodies of water do you find there?
> 6. Is the water fresh or salty?
> 7. What kinds of plants does the biome have?
> 8. Is there anything else that is important for others to know about your biome?
> 9. What Web site did you use for research?

6. Researching the questions above will carry into Day Three. After answering the questions, ask students to sketch a food web with the plants and animals of that biome, drawing arrows from predator to prey. Have *Who Eats What?* available for reference.
7. Ask your librarian or teaching partner to help students scan (or photograph) and save their webs and insert them into their wiki page.

Closure Ask each group to partner with another to share what they have learned. What do they have in common with their partner group's biome? What is different?

Assessment Review each wiki page for the accuracy and completeness of the notes and drawings. Work with individual groups as necessary to revise their work.

DAY FOUR (60 minutes): Animal Research
Launching the Lesson: Activating Prior Knowledge
Remind students of the biome notes and food webs they made.

Learning Activities

1. Say, "I'm glad we worked so hard to make those biome notes and drawings so accurate. Now that you've done that as a group, it's time to work by yourself. Choose one animal from your biome to research. Work with your group so that each of you has a different animal."

2. Ask students to create a new wiki page based on the template you have set up (see sample below or visit http://bit.ly/tsunami-links). Using the Web resources listed, as well as other librarian-recommended sources like PebbleGo.com or Go.Grolier.com, students research to learn about their animal, filling in Part One of the wiki page.

> 1. What is your name?
> 2. Who is your animal?
> 3. What are its predators?
> 4. What are its prey?
> 5. What plants does it eat?
> 6. What interesting things does it do?

Closure Ask students to work with their original biome group and compare animal notes.

Assessment Review the students' online notes for accuracy and completeness. Mini-conference as needed before moving to the next day.

DAY FIVE (60 minutes): Imagining Their Animal in A Different Biome
Launching the Lesson: Activating Prior Knowledge

1. Before class, write the name of each group's biome on four scraps of paper. Place them in a hat or box.
2. As students enter the room, ask them to draw a biome from the hat. (Select again if they receive their own biome.)
3. Remind students that yesterday, they learned a lot about their animal at home. In their adventure comic, their animal will travel to a different biome—the one they just selected—where the climate, food, and land will be different.

Learning Activities

1. Ask students to open the previous day's animal research in one tab or window and the appropriate class biome research wiki page in another. (Moving between tabs/windows is an important skill for budding researchers.)
2. They will use their colleagues' biome research to guide Part Two of their animal research page, where they will re-answer the Part One questions for the new biome. They may not find specific answers, so ask them, **"Do any of these animals seem bigger/ smaller than they are? Could they be predators/prey?"** This can help them use facts as a launching point for their imagination.
3. Then, ask them to fill out Part Three, answering these questions:

> 1. What is the same about your animal's home biome and the one it is visiting?
> 2. What is different about the two biomes?
> 3. What do you think your animal might eat in the new biome?
> 4. What animals might be predators of your animal?
> 5. Would your animal be cold or warm in the new climate?
> 6. What new things would your animal experience?
> 7. What story ideas are you getting?

Closure and Peer Assessment Ask students to partner-share emerging story ideas.

DAY SIX (30 minutes): Story Planning
Launching the Lesson: Activating Prior Knowledge
Remind students that they have been gathering all of this information to create an adventure story starring their animal.

Learning Activities Ask students to fill our Part Four of the wiki page, which asks them to name their animal, its friends, how the animal arrived in the new biome, the problems it will encounter, and how it will return home. Encourage them to refer to maps and globes to determine a path home.

Closure and Peer Assessment Ask students to find a new partner with whom to share progress.

DAYS SEVEN AND EIGHT (60 minutes each): Making Comics
Launching the Lesson: Activating Prior Knowledge
1. Ask students what they know about how comics are created. Allow them to browse some print or online examples (e.g., www.professorgarfield.org/toon_book_reader/).
2. Help students to see the key components of a comic: panels that contain each image, word balloons that show what characters are saying, thought balloons to show what characters are thinking, and narrative boxes that move the plot along.
3. Model the software you have chosen, showing students how the tool enables them to use panels and balloons to tell the story.
4. Model how to search for Creative Commons images if your tool does not have them built in (see Tsunami Tip below).
5. Using their brainstorming from their wiki page, students will use the software to tell the story of their character's surprise arrival in a new biome, what problems they face, and how to get home.
6. As students complete a draft of their comic, partner them so they can share feedback. Check their work against the previous step.
7. Students will upload a PDF of their comic (or add a link) to their animal research page. This page serves as documentation of their research, synthesis, and product.

Closure/Peer Assessment Invite students to view one another's work and leave constructive feedback on the Discussion tab.

Assessment Scoring should be based on group dynamics during the initial biome research, the completeness of the notes, the storyline, mechanics, and the use of CC-licensed photographs.

Extensions Invite students to turn their comics into radio plays. Share with other classes!

TSUNAMI TIP: Creative Commons Images
Many students believe that any online image (including Google Images) is okay to use in their project. That's not technically true: photographs are automatically copyrighted by the person who took the picture, even if it doesn't say it, which means you have to ask permission to use it. However, if someone gives their work a Creative Commons (CC) license, it means, "It's my work, but I give you permission to use it under certain circumstances." You can find CC images via Google's Advanced Search (click on the gear in the top-left corner to access it), http://flickrcc.bluemountains.net, http://flickr.com/creativecommons, or http://creativecommons.org (where you can learn more about the many kinds of CC licenses).

WHAT MAKES STATES UNIQUE?

Keywords: states, postcards, address formatting, linking words, travel
Kara Fribley and Eileen Thomas

Third graders are increasingly sophisticated problem solvers. They are also inquisitive and becoming stronger readers, writers, and researchers. In this lesson, students research and send a postcard from the state of their choice.

Key Standard

Writing 3.2—Write informative/explanatory texts to examine a topic and convey ideas and information clearly.

a. Introduce a topic and group related information together; include illustrations when useful to aiding comprehension.

b. Develop the topic with facts, definitions, and details.

c. Use linking words and phrases (e.g., also, another, and, more, but) to connect ideas within categories of information.

d. Provide a concluding statement or section

To accomplish this standard, students will need to be able to

- extract information and take notes from books and digital resources;
- with guidance and support from adults, produce writing in which development and organization are appropriate to the task and purpose (Writing 3.4);
- with guidance and support from peers and adults, develop and strengthen writing as needed by planning, revising, and editing (Writing 3.5); and
- determine the main ideas and supporting details of a text read aloud or information presented in diverse media and formats (from Speaking and Listening 3.2).

Time Needed

Four sessions of 45-60 minutes

Resources

Web sites (see http://bit.ly/tsunami-links)

Resource List

☑ United States map (virtual or physical)
☑ State brochures
☑ Books on the states (optional)
☑ Postcards
☑ Card stock
☑ Colored pencils, crayons, markers

DAY ONE (45–60 minutes): Introduction and Note Taking
Launching the Lesson: Activating Prior Knowledge

Using a digital or print map of the United States, ask students if they have traveled to any other states with their families. Allow students to give their answers and mark where they have traveled on the map. Now, ask students what they saw on their trips that was interesting and add those to the map using sticky notes or digital notes. Tell students that they are going to create postcards with interesting information about a state of their choice. If possible, invite someone from a local travel agency to come in and talk about what kinds of information they put in travel guides, and how they decide to include it.

Learning Activities

1. As a class, brainstorm what might make you want to visit a state. Prompt students by giving examples. You might say, "Do you want to go hiking in the mountains or swimming at the beach? Do you want to visit someplace warm or cold? Do you want to see national parks, cities, or wildlife? Do you want to try a particular type of food?"

2. Schedule time in the school library with your librarian. Have students visit the sites noted in the Resource List and (possibly) locate books on the states to look up information about states that they might be interested in. Allow time for your librarian to demonstrate and model any unfamiliar resources. Ask students to look at several states to find one that they would like to visit. Encourage students to sketch a Word web for note taking (see example).

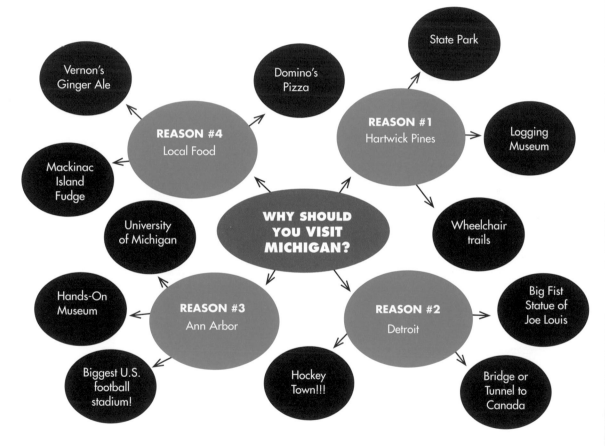

Closure Have students pair and share which states they chose and why.

Assessment Have students hand in their graphic organizer as an exit slip and check that each student has chosen a state.

DAY TWO (45–60 minutes): Research
Launching the Lesson: Activating Prior Knowledge

1. Tell students that this is their day to research what a visitor to their state would want to see and do. Ask them to vote (thumbs-up or thumbs-down) on which of these would interest them most in visiting the state next door: a water park, the colors in the state flag, the state rock, a science museum, the state bird, or the governor.
2. From this exercise, remind them of the kinds of information they are looking for in their research. A helpful Cloze sentence to help students evaluate whether information is helpful or not is:

> "Come to (state) because we have (fact)!"

3. Say, "If someone said to you, 'Come to Michigan because our state bird is the robin,' would you want to come? Of course not! But what if we said, 'Come to Michigan because we have hundreds of lakes where you can swim, build sand castles, go boating, lay in the sun, and waterski'? Absolutely!"

Learning Activities

Arrange a time to visit your school library so students can access resources on their states. Provide plenty of time for students to take notes and to test ideas against the Cloze sentence.

Closure Have students pair and share two interesting attractions they found in their state.

Assessment Ask students to hand in their graphic organizers so you can see their progress.

DAY THREE (60 minutes): Writing
Launching the Lesson: Activating Prior Knowledge

1. Bring postcards from your collection to class. (You could even ask the class's family members to send postcards to you in the months and weeks prior to the lesson!)
2. Show them to the class and discuss their structure—i.e., picture(s) on one side and writing on the other. Explain how and where postcards are addressed, including state abbreviations and ZIP codes.
3. Explain that they will be writing to invite a friend to join them on a road trip to the state they've chosen. Tell students to explain what they might do on that road trip. Model what you might say on a postcard using the state you're in based on a sample graphic organizer. Solicit ideas for using linking words and phrases (and, or, but, however, next, etc.; for more ideas, see page 74). Ask students to add detail to your example.

Learning Activities

1. Ask students to look again at their graphic organizers and add a bubble for Introduction and another for Conclusion. Then number each bubble in the order they will write about it. Brainstorm some possible introductions (e.g., "Hello from Rhode Island, a tiny state!" or "Greetings from Tennessee, the Volunteer State!") and conclusions (e.g., "The only thing that would make California better would be you! Love, Sam" or "There is so much to do in Michigan, so we should try to visit! See you soon! Juan"). Write these brainstormed sentences on chart paper and model how you would sequence the middle sentences using transition words.

2. Have students type the text for their postcard using a word-processing program set for two-columns in landscape format. Have students type their paragraphs and addresses.

3. After students finish typing, pair them up to partner-edit and make corrections on-screen. When you have checked their work, print the text on card stock.

Closure Ask students to close their eyes and imagine two or three pictures that would be great for their postcard front.

Assessment

☐ Is the address formatted correctly, including a zip code?
☐ Does the paragraph have an opening sentence that introduces the location?
☐ Are there at least three middle sentences with details that support the topic and begin with a linking word?
☐ Does the paragraph close with a concluding sentence that wraps everything up?

DAY FOUR (45 minutes): Finish Postcards
Launching the Lesson: Activating Prior Knowledge

Ask students to think back to the images they imagined on their postcard. Which would best illustrate their text?

Learning Activities

1. Ask students to brainstorm the best image and sketch it on scrap paper. Circulate among your students to check for progress and discuss image selection.

2. Ask students to share their sketches with you prior to drawing on their postcard with colored pencils, crayons, or markers! This is an excellent opportunity to collaborate with your art teacher!

Closure Have a few students read their postcards to the class each day. Display the postcards on a bulletin board. Use pushpins so visitors can easily view the other side.

Assessment Check the students' sketches for accuracy. As this project is assessed at each step, summative assessment may not be necessary.

Extensions Teach how to format a business letter. Encourage students to write to a state's tourism department for further information.

WHAT DO WE DO WITH THE STUFF WE DON'T WANT ANYMORE?

Keywords: environmental science, recycling, posters, announcements

Kara Fribley and Eileen Thomas

Third graders take a leap in confidence and reading fluency. They are interested in being active in the world around them. In this lesson, students engage in print, Web, and local community organizations to learn more about how they can reduce their environmental footprint.

Key Standard

Writing 3.8—Recall information from experiences or gather information from print and digital sources; take brief notes on sources and sort evidence into provided categories.

To accomplish this standard, students will need to be able to

- write informative/explanatory texts to examine a topic and convey ideas and information clearly (Writing 3.2);
- with guidance and support from adults, produce writing in which development and organization are appropriate to the task and purpose (Writing 3.4);
- determine the main ideas and supporting details of a text read-aloud or information presented in diverse media and formats, including visually, quantitatively, and orally (Speaking and Listening 3.2);
- extract information from informational texts and/or digital resources; and
- work effectively in groups.

Time Needed

Three 35-60 minute sessions

Resource List

☑ Reduce, Reuse, Recycle sign (download at http://bit.ly/recycling-sign)

☑ Paper and pencils

☑ Items for sorting (one set per group)
- Paper with one side used
- Empty plastic bottles, cans, and jars
- Paper with both sides used
- Cloth grocery bag
- Pictures of lightbulbs, water faucets, showers, toilets, disposable diapers, old chairs, clothes, dishes
- Styrofoam products
- Plastic utensils, cups, or plates
- Magazines
- Paperback or hardcover books

☑ Books
- *Kids Can Reuse* by Cecilia Minden (Cherry Lake, 2011)
- *Kids Can Recycle* by Cecilia Minden (Cherry Lake, 2011)
- *Save the Planet: Reduce, Reuse, and Recycle* by Cecilia Minden (Cherry Lake, 2010)
- *The Earth Book* by Todd Parr (Little, Brown, 2010)
- Additional recycling titles can be found on page 22

☑ Web sites
- Your city's local recycling information
- NIEHS Kids' Pages: Reduce, Reuse, Recycle at http://kids.niehs.nih.gov/explore/reduce/
- Pathfinder, wiki, or Web page listing URLs and/or phone numbers for local charitable organizations, libraries, recycling centers, and waste management

DAY ONE (45 minutes): Discarding Waste
Launching the Lesson: Activating Prior Knowledge

Ask your students if they have ever done anything for Earth Day. Write their answers down on a board or type them on a computer, and project them so everyone can see the answers. Now, show your students the Reduce, Reuse, Recycle sign. Ask them if they've seen a sign like it before and what it means to them. Ask them to "think, pair, share": First, think for a moment. Then exchange ideas with a partner. Finally, share their ideas with the entire class when prompted. As students share their definitions, write them down on chart paper. If students are unable to build correct definitions, give a mini-lesson on each.

Learning Activities

1. Bring out the bags of assorted objects that you collected (paper, bottles, cloth grocery bags, etc.). Divide the class into five groups. Give each group a bag. Say that all of the things in the bag are no longer needed at your house. Ask them, at tables or on the floor, to sort the items inside according to how this item should be used next. To help the environment, should it be used less (reduced), used again (reused), donated to a charity (which is a kind of reuse, but with someone else using it), recycled, or put in the trash? They may not agree right away, but they need to discuss each item until they reach consensus.
2. Use a timer like online-stopwatch.com to give your students 15 minutes to sort the objects. Tell students to write down which objects they placed in each category and why. This activity will allow you to determine your students' current level of understanding about each term.
3. Once the time is up, have the groups share what objects they put in each category and why. Record what the students agreed and disagreed about. Some items could be sorted in different ways. For example, a family that enjoys making things might reuse a magazine by turning it into a craft project. Another household might put it in the recycling bin. A third household might donate it to a charity like the public library or a thrift store. In this exercise, there are many possible answers!

Closure Talk through any discrepancies between groups as to where objects were placed. Clarify whether differences in sorting represent right, wrong, or merely different decisions. In real life, we handle items differently in our individual households. The important takeaway is that we not put items in the trash unless, like diapers or used tissues, it would be unsanitary, unhealthy, or unpleasant to do anything else with them.

Assessment Photograph each group's work as evidence of understanding. After class, print out the photographs and post them in the classroom or library.

DAY TWO (35–45 minutes): Research
Launching the Lesson: Activating Prior Knowledge

Remind students about how they sorted the objects during the last lesson and point out the photographs documenting their progress. Tell them that today, you'll be going to the school library to get some help from the librarian in gathering information about reducing, reusing, and recycling. Go down to the library and give students back their papers from the previous day.

Learning Activities

1. Have students divide into the same groups they were in for the first part of the lesson. Assign each group one category: reduce, reuse, recycle, trash, or donate. With the help of your school librarian, have enough resources for each group to research their category. Use books and Web sites such as those on the Resource List, as well as your premade list of Web addresses and phone numbers for the local library, waste management agency, recycling center, and thrift shops. Allow time for your school librarian to acquaint the students with any unfamiliar resources.
2. Provide each group with paper and pencils, and give students time to gather information. Their notes, which can be recorded on paper or on a wiki page, may include a list of tips (e.g., the Reduce group will have strategies for water reduction) or a list of what items can or cannot be included in their disposal category (e.g., the Donate group may discover that the thrift shop does not accept computers as donations). At the bottom of the page, ask students to write down the title and author of each book they consult and the URL of each Web page they use.
3. Have the groups report their findings. Record the definitions they found for reducing, reusing, and recycling, as well as the activities they can do for each.

Closure Call the group together. Ask each to share one surprising discovery.

Assessment Collect the notes taken by students during their information gathering as an exit slip.

DAY THREE (60 minutes): Posters
Launching the Lesson: Activating Prior Knowledge

Remind students of the information they gathered the previous day and revisit what they have learned. Yesterday, they were learners, but today, they will create posters to teach others.

Learning Activities

1. Talk to students about what makes an effective poster. Perhaps take a tour of the school to look at other posters. What makes them want to look at a poster? Possible areas to consider include simple, bold design (not too many fonts or competing graphics), short text, large fonts, and a bold, clear illustration so that it can be understood from a distance.
2. Use software such as Kidspiration, Kid Pix, TuxPaint, or PowerPoint to create a "Did you know?" Web page, slide, or poster sharing what they learned. Their poster should have at least three sentences: an attention-grabbing introduction, at least three supporting sentences, and a sentence encouraging people to take action. They should accompany their text with an appropriate illustration or clip art, depending on the software available. Model this on the board. For example:

Did you know that you don't have to throw away empty food cans? Wow! There are so many other things you can do! You could put them in your recycling bin. You could also cover them with paper to turn them into pencil holders. Everybody needs a place to put their pencils! So stop! Think before you trash!

3. For maximum impact, ask each student to work alone or make multiple copies of each group's printout.

Closure Ask students to trade screens and offer helpful feedback about content, writing style, and spelling. Spot-check students' work and offer feedback before they print. Hang the posters in the hallways and lunchroom of the school.

Assessment Consider these areas for assessment, using a check-plus, check, or check-minus system, or your home district's scoring code:

Rubric

Aesthetics
☐ The poster uses a font style and size that is easy to read.
☐ The poster has an illustration that supports the ideas in the paragraph.

Writing
☐ The poster has an introductory sentence.
☐ The poster has at least one sentence of details that support the introduction.
☐ The poster ends with advice for the reader.
☐ The poster gives accurate information and advice about waste management.
☐ Capitalization, spelling, and punctuation were corrected before printing.

Work Skills
☐ You used your time wisely.
☐ You worked well with your group.
☐ You contributed fairly to the group.

Extensions Have students write scripts for PA announcements during the week of Earth Day. Include practical suggestions for how their classmates could help save resources. Experts make great resources for research projects! Consider inviting representatives from local organizations to join your students while they research.

TSUNAMI TIP: Finding Specific Words on a Web Page
Looking for a specific word on a page? Type Ctrl+F in any browser, then the word you're looking for. Your browser will point out each place on the page where that word appears. It's not perfect (if you're looking for the word cat, the page won't find synonyms like kitten), but it will speed up your search!

Grade 4
HOW DOES A NATURAL DISASTER CHANGE THE EARTH'S SURFACE AND IMPACT PEOPLE?

Keywords: natural disasters, weather, climate, media literacy, sequencing, news stories
Ann Truesdell

Fourth graders are becoming ready for more advanced research, and they enjoy research that has a purpose. In this lesson, students research while wearing the hat of a reporter. The goal is to write a report in newspaper style or as a presentation.

Key Standard

Writing 4.2—Write informative/explanatory texts to examine a topic and convey ideas and information clearly.

a. Introduce a topic clearly, and group related information in paragraphs and sections; include formatting (e.g., headings), illustrations, and multimedia when useful to aiding comprehension.

b. Develop the topic with facts, definitions, concrete details, quotations, or other information and examples related to the topic.

c. Link ideas within categories of information using words and phrases (e.g., another, for example, also, because).

d. Use precise language and domain-specific vocabulary to inform about or explain the topic.

e. Provide a concluding statement or section related to the information or explanation presented.

To accomplish this standard, students will need to be able to

• use encyclopedia articles and online databases for research;

• highlight and extract relevant information from informational texts; and

• decipher the meaning of new vocabulary using clues from the text or by seeking a definition in a dictionary/glossary.

Time Needed

At least seven sessions

Resource List

☑ Encyclopedia articles on the following topics: landslides, earthquakes, and volcanoes. Check with your librarian to find out which encyclopedia your school subscribes to. Print copies of these articles (one article per student on the natural disaster being researched) to facilitate the note-taking lesson later in the unit.

☑ Books such as:
  • *A Changing Earth* by Heather Miller (Cherry Lake, 2009)
  • *Real World Math: Natural Disasters* series (Cherry Lake, 2012)

☑ Online database that can access newspaper articles and/or magazine articles (see suggestions at http://bit.ly/tsunami-links)

☑ Newspaper article graphic organizers, such as the ones at www.enchantedlearning.com/newspaper

DAY ONE (60 minutes): Introduction
Launching the Lesson: Activating Prior Knowledge

1. Begin by having the class watch a short news report about a natural disaster (see suggestions at http://bit.ly/tsunami-links).

2. After the video(s), ask the students what stood out in their minds. What did they learn about this particular disaster? You might call on a few students to share their initial impressions.

3. Ask the students the following questions, then watch the video again while they look for these points.

☐ How did the reporter behave?
☐ Which facts were given at the beginning of the video?
☐ Which facts were not given until the end of the video?
☐ What kinds of images did they see?
☐ What background information on the type of the disaster was given, if any?

4. Discuss the questions above as a class. You are dissecting what components are common to this type of news report. Make a list as a class. Guide students to include ideas such as:

- The most important information is given first (who, what, where, when, why, how), followed by less important facts like historical comparisons.
- Many news stories conclude with what can or is being done to help.
- The images showed the event in action, people being affected, and/or the aftermath.
- All have captions (called chyrons) at the bottom of the screen that give a brief description of the image, event, or location.
- The tone was serious when it involved peoples' lives, but was a bit more "peppy" when it was just a "cool phenomenon of nature" that didn't hurt anyone.

5. Say, "For this next project, you will be news reporters. Each of you will be in charge of preparing and reporting on a natural disaster that has occurred. It may be an earthquake, a volcano eruption, or a landslide. These are all geological disasters, or disasters that are caused in some way by movement of the earth's crust. You will be reporting on a real disaster, but before we get to that part, we have to understand that type of disaster thoroughly. We want to understand why these disasters happen and what the effects of the disaster might be. We need to gather background information. Let's begin!"

Learning Activities

1. Give students a paper copy of the encyclopedia article on their topic. Explain that an encyclopedia article contains the most important, basic information on a topic, so it's a good place to get started, learn key words, and get a beginning understanding of a topic.
2. Ask students to read through the article one time without taking any notes or highlighting anything. This will help students to focus on the topic and have some of the facts before going through and sorting the information. (You may want to pair students and have them take turns reading the article aloud, especially for students who may not be your best readers.)
3. Ask students to read the article again, individually, but this time highlight information that fits in the graphic organizer (page 59)—or write these questions on the board to help guide students. Model how to color-code the highlighting so that students categorize which highlighted note belongs to which question. Suggest that your students make a "key" at the top of their paper, such as:

Note-Taking Key	
Basic information	yellow
Causes	pink
Effects on the land	green
Effects on people	blue

In addition, have students circle new words or words that seem special/specific to this topic. For example, earthquake researchers might circle the words "seismograph," "faults," and "tremors."

Closure and Student Self-Assessment

Have students with the same topic/article pair and compare what they highlighted. Was anything missed? Did anyone highlight too much? If so, have those students decide what's really important (perhaps by underlining a few key items or writing in the margins).

DAY TWO (45 minutes): Paraphrasing and Note Taking
Launching the Lesson: Activating Prior Knowledge

1. The teacher or librarian should begin the day by teaching students how to paraphrase the information that they found yesterday. Point out that paraphrasing is the act of rephrasing someone else's words using your own words. If we want to show that we have used an author's exact words, either from the Web or print text, we use quotation marks.
2. Model paraphrasing. Show and read a section of one of the articles together, then remove the article from everyone's view (including your own) and show how you write it in your own words, without looking at the original words. Then check your words against the author's words to make sure that they are not too similar but that your facts are still correct.
3. Remind students that notes do not necessarily have to be in full sentences, but they should be complete thoughts.
4. Remind students that paraphrased notes often seem longer than what the author originally wrote. That's okay! This shows that you are explaining the information to yourself and that you really understand it.

Learning Activities

Now have students paraphrase their highlighted notes into a graphic organizer (page 59). Remind them to pay attention to how they categorized their notes!

Closure In the last five minutes, have students pair up with another student who is researching the same topic. Have them compare their paraphrased notes. Ask them to consider the questions below, confer with their partner, and make any necessary changes before completing for the day. For assessment purposes, perhaps have students make changes to their organizers in another color.

- Are there any words on your partner's graphic organizer that sound too much like the author's words?
- Did your partner miss any important facts?
- Did your partner miss any key words on the topic? Do you agree with his/her definitions of the new words?

Assessment Teachers may wish to collect the graphic organizers to use them for a midway assessment. Do students seem to understand the information? Is it explained effectively in their own words?

DAY THREE (45 minutes): Research
Launching the Lesson: Activating Prior Knowledge

1. Say to students, "It's time to examine a real-life earthquake, volcano, or landslide. Where do you go to read about real-life events?" Students might guess that people read about current real-life events in a newspaper or magazine, online, or in print. Events that happened awhile ago might have a book written about them.

Name: _____

Main topic (type of natural disaster): _____

Resource used for these notes: _____

Subtopic	Your Notes	New words & their meanings
Basic/intro. info.		
Causes: why/when/ where does it occur?		
Effects on the earth (how it changes the land)		
Effects on people (how it changes their lives)		

From Navigating the Information Tsunami: Engaging Research Projects That Meet the Common Core State Standards, K-5. Cherry Lake Publishing, 2013.

2. The teacher or librarian should then introduce and demonstrate the resource that students will use to find articles about a specific natural disaster.

Learning Activities

1. Students should find two to three articles on the same natural disaster (for example, a student researching earthquakes might find three articles on the January 2010 earthquakes in Haiti).
2. If possible, have students take their notes onto sticky notes. Only one note should be on each sticky, and it certainly helps if students indicate which of the points (below) the note addresses. For example, a student might write "Who – the fires from the earthquake wounded 40+ people." If sticky notes are not available, you might also use index cards or cut-up paper, stored in an envelope so they will not scatter.

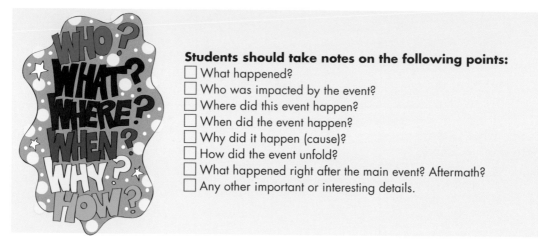

Students should take notes on the following points:
- ☐ What happened?
- ☐ Who was impacted by the event?
- ☐ Where did this event happen?
- ☐ When did the event happen?
- ☐ Why did it happen (cause)?
- ☐ How did the event unfold?
- ☐ What happened right after the main event? Aftermath?
- ☐ Any other important or interesting details.

Closure Ask students to turn to a peer and describe what they know thus far about the real-life disaster they are researching. Ask them to consider what similarities and differences their events have.

Formative Assessment Review the students' notes to assess their progress. Do students have enough information to write their own script? If not, you may want to schedule an extra day of research and note taking before moving on to Day Four.

DAY FOUR (45 minutes): Sequencing Notes
Launching the Lesson: *Activating Prior Knowledge*

1. Start the day by asking students, "Think about the news articles you read yesterday when you were researching. What did you notice about how news articles are written? How are they different from a book, encyclopedia article, or magazine article that you might read?"
2. Many students will probably note the length of the articles compared to books or even longer magazine articles. Try to guide students to seeing how the structure of a news article is different. "News articles put the most important information first. They are like an upside-down triangle: First, important facts, like the 5 Ws and a hook—an exciting introduction—to make people want to read more. Next, there is additional information about the event that people probably would want to know. The end is filled with the smallest details, things that could easily be cropped out if there is not enough space for the entire article."

Learning Activities

Students will take their sticky notes and arrange them on a large sheet of paper, poster board, bulletin, or butcher paper (that can be folded up between classes) to help them organize their news article. What information goes near the top? What notes are smaller details that can be left until the bottom? Visually, students should see how their news story will unfold. They may use a colored pen or marker to add in notes to help transition between stickies to identify places where they want to add more description or detail. For a variety of graphic organizers related to news writing, visit www.enchantedlearning.com/newspaper.

Closure and Peer Assessment Have students share their organized sticky notes with a peer. Ask them to describe the event to their peer, working from top to bottom. Encourage students to pay attention so that they can make suggestions about the notes' positions when necessary.

DAY FIVE (45 minutes): Writing a Rough Draft
Launching the Lesson: Activating Prior Knowledge

1. Start by showing the news videos of real-life disasters again (from Day One). Ask students to watch the video while looking for:

☐ Format—which information comes first?
☐ How are cause and effect linked?
☐ What background information is given on that type of disaster?
☐ Did the news anchor use any terms/words that are special or specific to that type of disaster?

2. Discuss what students found. Encourage them to keep these things in mind as they write their own news article.

Learning Activities

Students draft a news article using their organizers and these guidelines.

Articles should
- use the inverted-triangle format;
- use terminology and vocabulary appropriate to the topic, plus have the terms defined within the article as necessary; and
- tell about the real-life event (as if it recently happened) and give some background information on earthquakes/volcanoes/landslides in general, to help put the real-life disaster in perspective for the readers.

Closure Have a few volunteers share their drafts, so far, and point out examples of what criteria was well met and how other aspects could be improved. Use a data projector so students can see as well as hear the work.

Formative Assessment The teacher may also wish to collect the drafts to check for progress and identify a few anonymous examples for the next class session.

DAY SIX (45 minutes): Editing
Launching the Lesson: Activating Prior Knowledge

Using some anonymous samples (or made-up samples that have common mistakes the students are making), model how changes can be made so that the article is improved. For example, the teacher might show how to define a term within the article so that the definition is "worked in" briefly and clearly, without being too formal.

Learning Activities

Have students trade drafts with a partner to proofread. Encourage students to look at the criteria for their articles and make suggestions that are polite but essential.

Closure Ask students to make any necessary changes when they get their work back from their partner.

Formative Assessment Review the drafts overnight for progress.

DAY SEVEN (45 minutes): Finishing the Final Draft
Launching the Lesson: Activating Prior Knowledge

As you ask students to embark on finalizing the draft of their news article, you might want to share that most newspaper reporters have to do their rough draft, editing, and final draft all within a couple of hours to make it to print on time! If you are a writer for an online publication, maybe even sooner! Imagine how this would affect your writing!

Learning Activities

Students will write the final draft of their news article.

Closure Ask a few students to read their reports to the class as if they were news anchors. See if students can find any similarities and differences between the disasters, of both the same and different types.

Assessment Students should turn in all of their work from this project as a packet. Teachers will assess students using their highlighted article, their organized sticky notes, and both their rough and final drafts of the news article that they wrote. In particular, teachers will want to evaluate if students can

- extract information from multiple sources and compile it in a logical, organized manner;
- reorganize the information in a news report format, deciphering between the essential, basic, and less important facts; and
- introduce new vocabulary correctly within their own writing.

Extensions This project could easily be extended if teachers decided to have students turn their articles into a news broadcast. If students are using video as their broadcast medium, they might also want to gather images or video to be used in the video or as a "green screen" background. Broadcasts could be posted to YouTube or a wiki page to be shared with other students.

HOW IS AN ENDANGERED ANIMAL'S LIFE CYCLE AND/OR ECOSYSTEM AFFECTED BY PEOPLE? WHAT CAN PEOPLE DO TO PROTECT THIS ANIMAL FROM EXTINCTION?

Keywords: endangered species, public service announcements, activism, citation, animals

Ann Truesdell

Fourth graders are becoming ready for research that involves multiple resources, note taking, and considering how ideas connect. They enjoy research that has a purpose. In this lesson, students research an endangered animal to find why its existence is threatened and what they can do. They will share their findings with others in the form of a public service announcement.

Key Standards

Writing 4.7—Conduct short research projects that build knowledge through investigation of different aspects of a topic.

Writing 4.8—Recall relevant information from experiences or gather relevant information from print and digital sources; take notes and categorize information, and provide a list of sources.

To accomplish these standards, students will need to be able to

- paraphrase informational text;
- synthesize information to decide what is most relevant and persuasive in order to define a problem and suggest potential solutions to the problem; and
- search an online encyclopedia and/or database, then both read and skim for relevant information.

Time Needed

Six sessions

Resource List

☑ Web resources (see list at http://bit.ly/tsunami-links)

☑ Variety of printed books (one on each animal being researched if possible), plus:

- *Save the Planet: Helping Endangered Animals* by Rebecca Hirsch (Cherry Lake, 2010)
- *Road to Recovery* series, showing how once-endangered animal populations are rebuilding (Cherry Lake, 2009)

DAY ONE (60 minutes): Introduction and Note Taking
Launching the Lesson: Activating Prior Knowledge

1. Show students several public service announcements (PSAs) about endangered animals (see a list at http://bit.ly/tsunami-links) and read *Save the Planet: Helping Endangered Animals* (placing the book under a document camera for maximum visibility).
2. Invite students to discuss:

   ☐ Why were those commercials made?
   ☐ What does PSA mean?
   ☐ What does it mean if an animal is endangered?
   ☐ Why do we care if an animal is endangered?
   ☐ What happens if they are extinct?
   ☐ What are some reasons animals might be endangered?
   ☐ Are there things that people can do to prevent these animals from becoming extinct?

3. Based on your library's print and online resources, show students a list of endangered animals. Ask students to choose an endangered animal that they will each (or in pairs) research and then create their own PSA about.

			How is this affectd by threats to the animal?	
Topic	Endangered animal			
Background information	Life cycle			→
	Natural habitat (ideal ecosystem)			→
	Food web (including both predators and prey)			→
Focus on endangered status	How many of this species are left? Compare to numbers in the past.			
	What is the biggest threat to this animal's survival as a species?			
	Why does this threat exist?			
	What can be done to protect this animal from extinction?			

From Navigating the Information Tsunami: Engaging Research Projects That Meet the Common Core State Standards, K-5. Cherry Lake Publishing, 2013.

Learning Activities

1. Introduce the research graphic organizer (page 64) to the students. Explain how the organizer helps to structure the research. Students start by building background information about the animal (life cycle, food web, habitat), so that they can fully understand why it is endangered and what can be done to help.

2. Next, have the school librarian introduce a first resource to the students. A good place to start researching some basic information about a topic is an encyclopedia. Online encyclopedias have numerous features, including maps, photographs, and fast facts that can be helpful to students doing their early research. The librarian can highlight the features of the encyclopedia that will be most helpful to students, such as particular animal-related databases, searching tips, and how to choose the right article. (PebbleGo.com and Go.Grolier.com's Amazing Animals of the World are two good subscription options.)

3. The librarian or teacher will model how to extract information and take notes on the graphic organizer. Notes should be paraphrased (in the students' own words; see previous lesson), should be concise (complete sentences are not necessary), and may even contain drawings (such as a diagram of a food web).

4. Finally, invite students to find, read, and take notes using an article about their animal. If the articles are short or easy to read, have students read through the article once before reading it through a second time and taking notes. Note taking in the margins of a printout can help develop summarization and synthesis skills.

Closure and Formative Assessment In the last five minutes, gather back together and have students share what they have found.

1. What keyword did you use to search the online encyclopedia? Did you find an article right away?
2. Did the information you needed seem to jump out at you, or did you need to read carefully?
3. What features of the encyclopedia helped you to find the information you needed?
4. What did you learn about your animal? What did the beginning of the article say?

DAY TWO (45 minutes): Citation
Launching the Lesson: Activating Prior Knowledge

1. The teacher or librarian should begin the day by asking students if they know what it means to cite a source. "Why do we cite sources at the end of our research? We cite sources because we want to give credit to the people who did the original research and writing. We used their ideas and information that they found to do our work. Giving credit to them is like saying thank you—much like the credits at the end of a movie or television show, which list who worked on that production. It also helps you to find the resource again if you need to look up additional information or double-check your notes." Depending on the time you can allot to this, you may discuss plagiarism, academic dishonesty, and copyright with students as well, emphasizing the importance of recognizing others and not, at this age, the punitive perspective.

2. Model the process of note taking using the graphic organizer once more to refresh students' memories. This time, after you paraphrase an idea, write a "1" after the fact and perhaps circle it to make it stand out. Demonstrate how you then fill out the information in the second graphic organizer on page 66, to show which source you used.

Learning Activities

1. Pass out the citation graphic organizer below and cite the online encyclopedia along with the students. Model how you are finding the information from the site. Encourage students to fill in their citation forms along with you.

2. Invite students to continue reading and note taking. Finish using the online encyclopedia, then invite students to explore other resources as well (see Day Three).

Source Number	Title	Author	Year	Publisher or URL
1				
2				
3				
4				

Closure and Peer Assessment

During the last five minutes, have students trade notes and citation organizers, and ask them to double-check the others' notes for proper citations in each place. Fix any errors before leaving. As an "exit slip," have the students turn in their notes and citation organizers so that you can quickly assess their note-taking skills, citations, and how far they have come with their research.

DAY THREE (45 minutes): Gathering Further Information
Launching the Lesson: Activating Prior Knowledge

Point out to students that online encyclopedias, like the ones they used yesterday, are great starting points for finding information. But what if you need more than the basics? Encourage students to look at other resources and shift their focus from the background information to the threats about the animal. Students might use books or Web sites selected by the teacher or librarian or subscription databases. Ask your librarian for ideas.

Learning Activities

Today is for information gathering. Students will continue to move between citing sources on their references graphic organizer and taking notes on their note-taking graphic organizer. Make sure students are aware that they should also focus on how the life cycles, food webs, and habitats of their animals have been affected, if at all, by the same threats that are causing their endangerment.

Closure/Self-Assessment

Before leaving, briefly have students pair with another student and share which resources have worked best for their research.

DAY FOUR (45 minutes): Continuing to Gather Information
Launching the Lesson: Activating Prior Knowledge

Remind students that today is the last day for research. Encourage them to try the resources their peers told them about last class!

Learning Activities

Students continue to research as the teacher and librarian circle the room to give feedback and check for progress and understanding. Remind students to cite their sources!

Closure and Peer Assessment

In the last five to 10 minutes of class, have students gather to share, in small groups, what they discovered about their animal. Ask them to consider if there are any common reasons why animals seem to be endangered, then have a "reporter" from each group share the most common threat that their group discovered.

DAY FIVE (45 minutes): Scripting PSAs
Launching the Lesson: Activating Prior Knowledge

1. Review what students have accomplished and what they are working toward: a PSA to make others aware of why their animal is endangered and what people can do to help. Discuss the features of a PSA that draw in the audience and encourage them to take action, including:

Celebrity	Message	Images	Music	Tone

2. Next, discuss the three elements of a good PSA:

Problem: Tell your audience what the concern or problem is (the reason for your PSA).
Persuasion: Appeal to the audience's emotions and make them care about the problem. Educate them with effective facts and statistics.
Solution: Tell your audience what they can do to help. Be concrete and specific!

Learning Activities

Ask students to outline, then, script their PSA according to these three elements. Post the list so students can refer to them.

Closure/Peer Assessment Have students share their scripts with another student. Perhaps have your students read to their partner while the partner mentally (or literally) checks off whether all three criteria have been covered in the script. If the problem, persuasion, and solution are not obvious to the partners, some editing will probably be necessary.

DAY SIX, AND CONTINUING UNTIL PROJECT IS COMPLETE: Creating PSAs

1. To create a technology-based PSA, students may choose one (or you might assign) a technology medium with which to create their PSA, such as:

*   A digital poster at http://edu.glogster.com
*   Video commercial using an image slide show (e.g., Photo Story) or video footage edited in software such as iMovie or Windows Movie Maker
*   An audio commercial made with software such as Audacity (http://audacity.sourceforge.net) or Garage Band

2. Remind students to cite where their information (and pictures, if using any) came from, ideally at the end of their PSA.
3. Students will work each day until the project is complete. If time is limited, this step may be omitted, and students can move directly to the oral presentation noted below.

FINAL DAY: Sharing Projects

Students should view one another's PSAs in some format. You could hold a "screening" where the whole class watches each video or listens to each "radio" commercial. Another idea is a "musical chairs" sharing, where students each open up their project on a computer and then students circle around the room to view each other's projects. Alternatively, students could post their final project to a wiki, and each student could visit the others' pages to view the projects. If a technology project is not created, consider oral presentations of their scripts.

Closure After students have seen each other's PSAs, revisit the common reasons that different animals are endangered. What effect will this have on humans? How will it modify their ecosystems? Look for better student understanding of the impact of these animals becoming extinct. Compare to earlier discussions.

Assessment Teachers will want to grade/assess students on all parts of the project.

- ☐ On the graphic organizers, was information accurate, paraphrased effectively, and categorized correctly?
- ☐ Did students cite their sources correctly both on the citation organizer and in their final PSA?
- ☐ Did students' scripts and final projects showcase understanding of the threat to their animal and possible solutions, while effectively persuading the audience?
- ☐ Did the students use relevant facts to effectively describe the problem, identify a solution, and persuade the audience to take action?
- ☐ Were textual mechanics strong according to Common Core conventions guidelines?

Extensions There are many directions in which teachers can take this lesson. The research skills can be applied to any research lesson, the graphic organizers might be adapted for other topics, and PSAs can certainly be used by students to show their learning on a variety of subjects. A favorite way to adapt this lesson is to focus on local ecosystems and the different threats present in each. Students discover what is happening close to home and consider what they themselves can do to help solve the problem.

*The Day Six activities were originally designed by Raya Samet, now with the Hawken School in Ohio.

HOW DOES THE TRUE STORY OF THE FIRST THANKSGIVING COMPARE TO OUR MODERN INTERPRETATIONS OF THE EVENT?

Keywords: myths, American history, holidays, misconceptions

Ann Truesdell

Fourth graders can understand the difference between fact and fiction, and between fact and fiction that could have been true. They can understand how evidence might be used to prove something as fact, while details in a story can make things sound like they could have really happened. In this lesson, students talk about the "Thanksgiving Myth" and what really happened at that fall festival long ago. They use both informational texts and literature to dig deeper into fact versus fiction of that "legendary" event.

Key Standard

Writing 4.9—Draw evidence from literary or informational texts to support analysis, reflection, and research.

To accomplish this standard, students will need to be able to
- discuss the difference between fact/fiction, true/false, and reality/make-believe;
- navigate Web sites, including multiple Web sites at the same time; and
- use a variety of techniques to find and extract information from informational texts.

Resource List
☑ Sticky notes
☑ Student writing journals
☑ Web resources from http://bit.ly/tsunami-links
☑ Supplemental informational texts about Thanksgiving and Plimouth Plantation, such as:
- *America's Colonization and Settlement* by Marcia Amidon Lüsted (Cherry Lake, 2011)
- *Thank You, Sarah: The Woman Who Saved Thanksgiving* by Laurie Halse Anderson, illustrated by Matt Faulkner (Simon & Schuster, 2002)

Time Needed
Three to four sessions of 60-75 minutes each

DAY ONE (60–75 minutes; may also split this into two days): What is true about the first Thanksgiving?
Launching the Lesson: Activating Prior Knowledge
1. Have the classroom set up with a projector and computer, plus three large poster boards or sections on the wall, one each labeled "Maybe True," "Myths," and "Truths." Be prepared with sticky notes.
2. Ask students to close their eyes and visualize how they celebrate Thanksgiving for a moment. Ask students, "How many of you celebrate with a turkey?" A number of students will likely raise their hands. "How many of your families watch football? Do you take turns sharing what you are thankful for? How many of your families get together with extended family or friends, too? What decorations do you set out?" Have students raise hands or give short answers.
3. Ask students to close their eyes again, and this time, create a picture in their mind of how they see the first Thanksgiving—that one with the Pilgrims and Native Americans back in the olden days. Now, pass out a small stack of sticky notes to each student and ask them to write down some of the things they pictured happening. (For assessment purposes, have the students write their names or initials on the back of the notes.) Prompt students to make notes on what different people wore, what they ate, how they celebrated, who was there, how long the event went on for, where they were, why the event took place,

etc. As students finish writing, have them take turns bringing their sticky notes to the "Maybe True" board. If there are any duplicates, stack them or group them close together.

4. When students have finished posting notes, read them aloud to the students. "I see that many people put that there was a large feast with turkey and potatoes. The Native Americans were invited by the Pilgrims because they had been so helpful and they were thankful to be friends. The celebration took place at the end of November. They were in Plymouth, Massachusetts. ..." Assure students that they seem to know many facts about Thanksgiving, but that many facts are not quite true. Much of what we think we know about Thanksgiving is myth, legend, or stereotype. Through research and reading like a historian, students will uncover the truth of the first "Thanksgiving Day."

Learning Activities

1. As a class (with the help of a projector so that everyone can see), visit Scholastic's Voyage on the Mayflower Web site (www.scholastic.com/scholastic_thanksgiving/voyage/). Together, explore the "Take the Journey," "Tour the Ship," and "Timeline" modules together.

2. Model how to take notes on a sticky note and put it on the correct board. For example, you might write down "The Pilgrims set sail for Plymouth, MA" on a sticky note and add it to the "Maybe True" board.

3. Then, model your thinking aloud to the class: "I always thought that this was what happened, but I learned from this Web site that the Pilgrims were actually sailing to Virginia, not Massachusetts. They got blown off course by a storm and ended up landing in Cape Cod, Massachusetts, then moved to Plymouth. I will add my sticky note about sailing to Plymouth to the 'Myths' board, and make a new sticky note citing what actually happened to put on the 'Truths' board."

4. Then, send students on their own or with a partner to explore the "Daily Life" and "The Thanksgiving Feast" sections. Give them their own sticky notes and encourage them to add thoughts they think might be true to the "Maybe True" board (for assessment purposes, put their initials on the back of their stickies). As students find out which thoughts are truths and which are myths, have them move their notes to the appropriate spots. With the note originator's permission, students may move others' notes as well. The catch is that students must add another note to the original with evidence from the text explaining the move to "Myths" or "Truths."

5. Gather the class together to discuss what has been learned. Which notes have been moved and to where? Do any more need to be moved onto the "Myths" or "Truths" boards? What new facts did we uncover? Are we still unsure about any of the notes on "Maybe True"?

Closure and Formative Assessment

1. Show *This Is America, Charlie Brown: The Mayflower Voyagers*, part 2 (http://youtu.be/fTYjwDOZqtQ) from 9:00 to the end (about two minutes total).

2. Discuss what inaccuracies students see now that they have uncovered evidence from today's resource. Jot down some of the myths and add them to the "Myths" board.

DAY TWO (60 minutes): Self-Paced Learning
Launching the Lesson: Activating Prior Knowledge

1. Ask students to review what they discovered about the myths and truths of Thanksgiving yesterday. Use the boards as a guide.

2. Together, read what remains on the "Maybe True" board. Tell students that their mission for the day is to be even more like a true historian and researcher.

Learning Activities

1. Ask students to work in pairs on Scholastic's Thanksgiving Web Quest (www.scholastic. com/scholastic_thanksgiving/feast/webquest.htm). For the first question, model how students will have to click on "visit the website" and choose the appropriate article to read. The students will have to peruse the article for facts that answer the Web Quest question. Review a couple of techniques to help students search within the article such as skimming (reading quickly through headings, words in bold font, and the first and last sentences of a paragraph) and using Ctrl + F or Command + F to find specific words on a page (see the Tsunami Tip on page 55).

2. As students move through the Web Quest, have them write more notes, again on sticky notes. They might write notes for any of the categories (Myths, Maybe True, or Truths). Encourage them to label or sort by category while they are taking notes so that they don't get too jumbled! Also, remind them to put their initials on the back. Have them keep all of their notes with them until most students are finished with the Web Quest; then have students take turns placing their notes on the appropriate boards.

Closure and Formative Assessment

1. As a class, review additions to all of the boards. Reorganize any notes that appear more than once so that they are grouped. Together, review what was a myth and verbally "correct" any myths with a fact from the "Truths" board.

2. Consider giving students an exit slip as they leave that shows, in writing, where they left off with the Web Quest. This could be indicative of their effort and/or ease in finding information. You might ask them to list one success and one frustration to help you understand their skill level. In addition, you can gather data from the notes that they contributed this day.

DAY THREE (60 minutes): Historical Fiction
Launching the Lesson: Activating Prior Knowledge

1. Ask students, "What is historical fiction?" If students are familiar with the genre, they may say something along the lines of "made-up stories that take place in the past." Discuss with students why some people might enjoy this genre (someone might suggest that they/others enjoy it because it teaches you a little bit about history). Point out to students that a key difference between history and historical fiction is that we know that historical fiction is fiction, even if it "seems" real. Many historical fiction authors use historically accurate settings, traditions, routines, events, and sometimes even people in their stories. However, historical fiction can also have invented characters or events that are plausible for the time period of the book. Historical fiction authors often do a lot of research to make sure their stories are representative of the time period.

2. Explain that today, students will be reading short pieces of historical fiction. The author of these fictional letters used research and evidence to try to make the letters seem as realistic as possible. He or she considered how the fictional characters would actually have felt if they were living during the 1620s in Plymouth, Massachusetts.

Learning Activities

1. As a class or in small groups, ask students to read four of Scholastic's "Plimoth Plantation Letters" (www.scholastic.com/scholastic_thanksgiving/letters.htm) about Autumn 1620 and Harvest 1621. Audio is available. All letters are historical fiction: two from the point of view of a Wampanoag child and two from the point of view of a Pilgrim child.

2. Using their knowledge from the previous days' activities, combined with what they gather and infer from the letters, ask students to individually answer the following questions in their journals. For each question, ask the students to provide at least two pieces of supporting evidence with their answer, one from the letters and the other from the past days' research. Encourage them to refer back to the boards showcasing the class's research notes.

Questions
- What happened at the Harvest Festival?
- How did the children feel about each other?
- What did the Pilgrims and the Wampanoags learn from each other?
- How does the Harvest Festival of 1621 compare to how you originally pictured the first Thanksgiving feast?
- How does the Harvest Festival of 1621 compare to your family's Thanksgiving traditions?

Closure Invite students to share their answers with each other or with the class. End by asking the overarching question: "Why does it matter if our view of the first Thanksgiving celebration was inaccurate? Why is it important to know the truth?"

Assessment Students' abilities to reflect and analyze the answers to the questions posed can be found in their journal entries from this day. Were the students able to cite evidence from their research and the historical fiction letters in order to support their answers?

Extensions
1. Students might want to further research the "real" first Thanksgiving. Consider having them use other books, articles, and Web sites for research. Students could dig deeper into what life was like in 1620 by further examining different aspects of life (eating, housing, childhood games, etc.) of both the Pilgrims and native people.
2. Students may also benefit from a final project in which they produce informational posters or a slide show about the myths versus historical facts.

TSUNAMI TIP: If YouTube Is Blocked at School
YouTube.com is a rich source of video resources, but it is often blocked by schools' filters. If unblocking the site is not an option, use a tool like zamzar.com or keepvid.com to download the video for later use. You can even download it in audio format so you can listen in the car on your way to work.

TSUNAMI TIP: READING DIGITALLY

The Common Core State Standards' assessments will be administered online. Are your kids fluent in digital as well as print reading skills? Unlike with print text, which we read linearly, our eyes tend bounce around the screen, skimming some lines and glancing at images before quickly moving on to another site. We must help our students learn to read in a sustained way in a digital environment and to employ deep thinking skills. Here are some sites that can help your students build this important muscle:

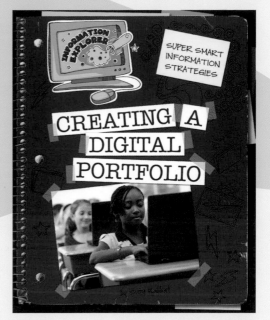

Readability.com can help kids and adults alike combat the visual overload of online content. Installed on a browser toolbar, Readability.com can strip away the superfluous elements, leaving just the text. This can help students, especially those who struggle to focus, to practice online reading with fewer distractions.

The International Children's Digital Library (en.childrenslibrary.org) gathers picture books in multiple languages from around the world and, with permission, scans them into their child-friendly search portal. Seeing familiar picture book layouts onscreen is an easy way for children to read age-appropriate texts online. Additionally, ICDL can be an important source of international texts to allow ELL children to read at home in their language of origin with their family.

Subscription Encyclopedias and Databases, paid for with school library, district, or state funds, are a great addition to your differentiation toolkit. Some database articles are leveled by Lexile or difficulty levels; can be auto-translated into multiple languages, which will help your ELL learners gain reading fluency in their own language while learning English; and can read the text aloud with mp3 files. These scaffolds can help all learners, but particularly those who struggle with reading.

TweenTribune.com pulls together middle-grade-friendly news stories (from pop culture to solar power to animals) and invites students to post feedback. This real-world setting helps kids read closely and practice developing arguments and supporting them with details. To keep kids safe, kids blog under aliases; teachers enroll their classes and moderate all submissions.

ImagineNation Matters is a web-based curricular activity (for grades 3-8) comprising over twenty interactive story modules that explore significant events and ideas in our nation's history (e.g., The Underground Railroad) and modern life (state government, healthy eating). On each page of their story, students are prompted with questions that frame opportunities to write for an audience, to think more deeply about the text, and to employ skills of empathy, observation and prediction. Undergraduate mentors from the University of Michigan respond to the students in the voice of the story characters, building on student engagement to encourage kids to further develop their ideas and to support their assertions with evidence. Visit http://umsimulations.wikispaces.com/ImagineNation+Matters to learn more.

Grade 5

HOW DO WE CREATE A PERSUASIVE ARGUMENT THAT IMPACTS OUR COMMUNITY?

Keywords: community issues, citizenship, persuasive writing

Emily Johnson and Jan Dohner

Fifth graders are often making an exciting transition between a self-contained classroom to working with different teachers during their school day. They are beginning to work on more long-term projects, which require more organizational skills. In this lesson, the students will examine an issue in their local community, research that issue, and write an editorial about how to solve the problem or improve the situation.

Key Standard

Writing 5.1—Write opinion pieces on topics or texts, supporting a point of view with reasons and information.

a. Introduce a topic or text clearly, state an opinion, and create an organizational structure in which ideas are logically grouped to support the writer's purpose.

b. Provide logically ordered reasons that are supported by facts and details.

c. Link opinion and reasons using words, phrases, and clauses (e.g., consequently, specifically).

d. Provide a concluding statement or section related to the opinion presented.

To accomplish this standard, students will need to be able to

- identify a community issue for which action is needed;
- research the issue in order to form an opinion supported by factual details; and
- send the opinion piece on to stakeholders in the form of an editorial or letter.

Time Needed

Four 60-minute sessions

Resource List

☑ Internet access

☑ A series of local newspaper editorials and/or letters to the editor about an issue that is relevant to your students. Ask your librarian to help you find examples that are written on your students' reading level.

☑ A curated list of local information resources (e.g., a local newspaper, the city or county Web site, community newsletters, school newsletters, etc), in print and/or electronic format. Having a premade online pathfinder or online list of links is typically easiest and can be used and maintained by multiple teachers. Again, ask your librarian for ideas!

☑ Persuasive Map graphic organizer from the National Council of Teachers of English, in print or interactive format (http://bit.ly/ncte-persuasion-map)

☑ A sample of a poorly written editorial (see page 77)

☑ Optional: access to Gale Opposing Viewpoints database (www.gale.cengage.com/InContext/viewpoints.htm). Try the read-aloud feature!

DAY ONE (60 minutes): Introduction
Launching the Lesson: Activating Prior Knowledge

1. Ask students how people voice their opinions about problems or situations in their local community. We are specifically looking for ideas that show how to influence people by writing to them, or presenting an argument that is based in fact—for example, debates, restaurant or movie reviews, editorials, or letters to government leaders.

2. Explain that for this assignment, they will choose an issue that has a direct impact on their everyday life and write an editorial that explains the issue, demonstrates why it is important, and persuades the reader to improve the situation or fix the problem.

Learning Activities

1. Define editorial (a persuasive argument written to influence others that may be printed in the newspaper, read on the radio, or shared on TV) and letter to the editor (a persuasive argument written in letter format to newspaper editors in hopes that the letter will be printed in the newspaper's print or online edition).
2. Display the local editorial or letter to the editor on a large screen. Explain to students that, like this sample, they will research an issue so that they can write a similar letter or editorial.
3. Display the NCTE Persuasive Map on-screen. As a class, work through filling it out, identifying the thesis, the key arguments, the evidence to back up the arguments, and the conclusion. Explain your thinking to the students and talk about the writer's intent in presenting the issue as he or she did. Ask the students to help identify what the writer believes should be done, what facts the writer uses to support that stance, and how the writer cites sources.
4. Divide students into groups of two to four, and distribute examples of editorials and opinion pieces, as well as print copies of the Persuasive Map. Ask groups to read the editorials and fill out the Persuasive Map. Walk around to observe and check for understanding.

Closure and Group Assessment

Leave some time at the end of the session for each group to share its findings with the class in 60-second explanations: the issue, what they felt the author was trying to persuade them to believe or do, and what evidence the author provided to support his or her claims. Gather graphic organizers at the end of class.

DAY TWO (60 Minutes): Researching in the Library
Launching the Lesson: Activating Prior Knowledge

1. This portion of the assignment is best done in the library. Work with the school librarian beforehand to help identify good resources or tools that students can use to research their topics, and to develop a curated list of local information resources that include online and print materials that may help them formulate their ideas.
2. Ask students if there is something going on in their community that has a direct effect on them or that they are really passionate about (e.g., a local bond election to buy new educational technology for school, a new ordinance banning skateboards from parks, a school rule that prohibits soda in school, zero-tolerance school rules, or seat belt ordinances). After students brainstorm a list, ask them to elaborate on the issue until they find a topic that can be summarized or discussed easily (for example, "Should our community have a parade for veterans now or when all veterans have returned home?" is manageable, whereas "Is the war just?" is too complex). Write their ideas on the board, for later reference.

Learning Activities

1. Remind students of their previous session, when they dissected the editorials.

2. Today, students will brainstorm and research an issue from the list that is important to them. Using the resources provided, students will research the issue, filling out the same Persuasive Map as a guide for their thinking. When their research is complete, they will write an editorial or letter to the editor.

3. Set a goal with students to identify and cite at least two sources. In some schools, students use NoodleTools.com to develop bibliographies.

4. Students will brainstorm on their own, using the class brainstorm as a guide. The topic needs to be approved by the teacher or librarian (to ensure that they are not overreaching their capabilities and to make sure that it is a relevant topic).

5. While they are researching, they should be filling out a new graphic organizer on their own. This will be used as a framework in the next session to begin writing their opinion piece.

6. Once they have a topic, students can use online and print resources from the premade list of links to find supporting facts for their arguments. Because the goal of this project is to focus on finding supporting evidence for their arguments, this lesson bypasses search. (However, see Tsunami Tip pages 93–94 for later practice with search strategies.)

Closure and Assessment About 10 minutes before the end of the session, ask students to share their research in small groups. Have them determine whether their peers have found resources that support their claims, whether they have made a persuasive argument with that evidence, and whether they can and need to do more research. If there is time, you could briefly discuss how they can do further research, such as interviewing someone who is knowledgeable about the subject. Their graphic organizers and peer evaluations are the ticket out of the class and give you the opportunity to formatively assess their learning.

DAY THREE (60 Minutes): Synthesis and Writing
Launching the Lesson: Activating Prior Knowledge

1. Meet in a computer lab, preferably one within or near the library, in case students need help finding or verifying their resources.

2. Begin the class by trying to "sell" students on a radical idea, such as increasing the length of the school day to 10 hours. Use facts to support your argument (e.g., having a longer school day will allow latchkey kids to get more adult supervision and homework help). Try to convince the students that your way is the best way! (Alternatively, show the first two minutes of this video: www.youtube.com/watch?v=fQ_cWPvtS8A. If YouTube is blocked at your school, see page 72.)

3. Ask them to share which arguments seemed the most persuasive and why. What can they take away from the sample and apply to their own work?

Learning Activities

1. Today, students will take their research and write their editorial (or letter to the editor). Google Docs (docs.google.com) is an easy way to draft work that can be shared during the editing process. Remind students of the examples they have looked at, the research they recorded on their Persuasion Map, and the ideas that they are passionate about. Circulate the room to help and mini-conference as needed.

2. After drafting their piece, students can revise their own work, then peer-edit with a partner.

Closure and Assessment At this point, students will have a rough draft of their opinion piece to print out. Their homework is to have someone outside of the school read and edit it. Remind students to focus on editing and revising the argument, not just the grammar.

DAY FOUR (60 Minutes): Revise and Connect
Launching the Lesson: Activating Prior Knowledge

1. Meet in a computer lab, preferably one within or near the library, in case students need help finding or verifying their resources.
2. Display the faulty editorial example below on a large screen. Ask the students to read through it and see what the problems are with the argument, tone, and writing. As a class, work through the editorial together, revising the arguments, decreasing the confusion, smoothing out the mechanics, and removing any ambiguity.

Learning Activities

1. Introduce the idea of transition words to students. These words can be placed at the beginning of a sentence or between two sentences to connect them.
2. Divide students into pairs. Have them read and revise one another's editorials, adding transition words. Allow students most of the time to work on their revision. When they are done, have them print or submit their documents (or, if using Google Docs, students can simply share their completed article with the teacher).

OUR AWFUL EXAMPLE

To the Editors:

You should defiantly change your vote. We need a skatborde park bad!!! They are cool! Tony Hawk is cool and famous. If you want us too be a cool city, vote for a skateboard park. Do it!!!!!!!!!

Love,

John Smith

Sample Transition Words

Sequencing words: First, Second, Third, Next, Finally
Words that signal a change or contrast is coming: However, In contrast to, A different
Words that explain how two ideas are related: As a result, Consequently, Specifically, Another, Similarly, For example, As an example

Closure Ask students what they should do with the editorials now that they are completed. Should they just file them away? Or could they actually send them somewhere to help make their voices heard? The response we are hoping to elicit is that students will decide to submit their editorials (or letter to the editor) to a local newspaper or magazine. Students can do this on their own, or the teacher could help them with the process.

Assessment Throughout the project, students have turned in their work-in-progress as an exit ticket so that they can get timely feedback about their learning and progress. The summative assessment of the student learning is the final editorial.

Extensions The beauty of this lesson is that students create a tangible outcome that they can share with real community stakeholders. This encourages them to participate in their local community and be unafraid to make their opinions known. If their piece is printed or they receive a response, share it with the class!

Assessment Checklist

The student:

☐ Selected a topic that is relevant to the local community.

☐ Introduced the topic clearly.

☐ Stated an opinion clearly.

☐ Gave reasons that supported the opinion.

☐ Used factual details from research to support the argument.

☐ Used transition words effectively.

☐ Ended with a conclusion that restated the desired action.

☐ Used and cited sources appropriately.

☐ Worked productively and used time wisely.

☐ Served as a helpful peer editor.

☐ Listened actively during instructional time.

☐ Participated in class discussion.

HOW DID THE GREAT DEPRESSION AND DUST BOWL AFFECT THE LIVES OF AMERICANS?

Keywords: photographs, primary sources, Dust Bowl, Great Depression, 20th-century history, personal narratives

Melissa P. Johnston

In fifth grade, students seek opportunities to prove themselves and tackle additional responsibility for independent learning. In this lesson, students will explore the Dust Bowl through video and both digital and print resources, then use primary source images to inspire a photo narrative. This project dovetails effectively with social studies exploration of 20th-century history, with a language arts unit on the Newbery Award–winning novel-in-verse *Out of the Dust*, or with a 21st-century unit on sustainability and the perils of poor sustainability practices.

Key Standards

Writing 5.3—Write narratives to develop real or imagined experiences or events using effective technique, descriptive details, and clear event sequences.

Writing 5.4—Produce clear and coherent writing in which the development and organization are appropriate to task, purpose, and audience.

Writing 5.5—With guidance and support from peers and adults, develop and strengthen writing as needed by planning, revising, editing, rewriting, or trying a new approach.

Writing 5.7—Conduct short research projects that use several sources to build knowledge through investigation of different aspects of a topic.

Writing 5.8—Recall relevant information from experiences or gather relevant information from print and digital sources; summarize or paraphrase information in notes and finished work, and provide a list of sources.

To accomplish these standards, students will need to be able to
- Use primary and secondary sources
- make inferences and draw conclusions;
- Sequence events using outlining or storyboarding;
- use narrative techniques, such as dialogue, description, and pacing;
- use rich vocabulary and sensory details to enliven narrative;
- demonstrate oral speaking skills;
- plan, revise, edit, and publish to demonstrate learning;
- keyboard efficiently (Writing 5.6 sets a goal of two pages per sitting); and
- use technology to search, find information, and communicate findings.

Time Needed

Five to seven days (combine blocks or periods to complete in fewer days)

Resource List

☑ Online resources
- Wiki-based graphic organizer
- Link to PBS American Experience video and transcript (http://bit.ly/tsunami-links)

☑ Print Resources
- *History Digs: The Great Depression and World War II* by Sheryl Peterson (Cherry Lake Publishing, 2012)
- *Go Straight to the Source!* by Kristin Fontichiaro (Cherry Lake Publishing, 2010)
- *Migrant Mother: How a Photograph Defined the Great Depression* by Don Nardo (Compass Point, 2011)
- Assorted nonfiction and reference books related to the topic (ask your librarian)

☑ Graphic Organizers
- Be a History Detective! sheet (page 81)
- Narrative writing graphic organizer (choose one from www.creativewriting-prompts.com/personal-narrative-graphic-organizer.html)
- Research graphic organizer
- Personal Narrative Project Rubric (pages 85-86)

DAY ONE: Introduction and Primary Sources
Launching the Lesson: Activating Prior Knowledge

1. Partner with your librarian for this lesson. Set the scene for the day by playing sounds of howling wind as they enter the library (try the free audio at bit.ly/tsunami-links). Students are invited to travel back in time to when there were no cell phones, computers, or Internet—a time when their family and their own survival depended on their quick thinking, hard work, and luck.

2. Show the PBS online video *The American Experience: Surviving the Dust Bowl* (http://bit.ly/tsunami-links; running time 52:31). This video is so compelling that students are engaged without needing a note-taking task.

Learning Activities

1. Just as the detectives on television need specialized tools, so do history detectives. The students now know something about how, when, and where people were hardest hit by the Dust Bowl, so they are ready to go out on their own and learn more. With the librarian, introduce the concepts of primary and secondary sources. Utilizing questioning strategies, evoke responses from students that explain the difference between primary sources (eyewitness) and secondary sources (based on eyewitness, but the creator was not present at the event), and note different examples of each. Ask the group, "Which tools would be useful in an investigation of the events and people of the Dust Bowl?" Note these on a whiteboard.

Examples of Primary Sources	Examples of Secondary Sources
Any of these can be primary sources if they were created during the Dust Bowl: • Letters • Diaries or journals • Photographs • Artifacts or objects • Interviews • Newspaper or magazine articles • Government documents	• Encyclopedias • Textbooks

2. Continue by saying, "As any good detective knows, there is always evidence left behind. The same is true of past times in history: there are clues left behind." Challenge students that their mission is to gather these clues, ask questions, and develop their own hypothesis, or educated guess, of what really happened.

3. The librarian can then introduce that today's mission is to learn to use photographs as clues. As image detectives, students will need to pose questions, gather clues, find information, and draw conclusions in order to answer the question: "What can we learn about history by looking at photographs?"

4. To demonstrate and model this process to students, project a Dust Bowl photograph (suggestions at http://bit.ly/tsunami-links). Give students a copy of the Be a History Detective! sheet below and model your thinking process. Alternatively, use the "See, Think, Wonder" method from page 8. Ask the librarian to scribe the students' responses.

5. Project a second image and ask students to respond with details they see in the photograph.

Be a History Detective!

All good detectives follow a process during their investigation. Your job is to investigate the clues left behind by the people of the Great Depression and Dust Bowl era. Use this organizer to help you analyze, understand, and interpret the photograph's clues.

Observe	Background Knowledge	Deductions
What do you see in this photograph? Make a list of the details you see.	What do you know about this time period from previous classes, reading, research, or your own experiences?	What conclusions can you draw or inferences can you make based on what you see in the photograph and your background knowledge? Make a list of your conclusions or inferences.

GRADE 5

6. Then tell students it is time to start their investigation. Explain that each group will have a photo to gather clues from, and they can record their information on the history detective sheet.
7. Break students into groups of four to five per table. Give each table a unique image (displayed on-screen or printed) and a graphic organizer. Working as a group, students will discuss, brainstorm, and fill in the columns. The teacher and school librarian will rotate around to each group to answer questions, give formative feedback, and stimulate discussion when needed.

Closure At the conclusion of the session, ask each group to share its photograph, the clues they found, and what they determined was happening. The teachers will share feedback as needed, ultimately revealing the citation and accompanying descriptive information (e.g., the setting and events of the photo).

Assessment The teaching team will observe and check for understanding via mini-conferencing at tables and the completed graphic organizers.

DAY TWO (60 minutes): Investigating Images
Launching the Lesson: Activating Prior Knowledge
As students enter the classroom, images from the Great Depression and the Dust Bowl will be projected (try http://youtu.be/vXqflrkJiO4). Remind students of the personal accounts they heard in the PBS video. Today, they will step into their photograph and give a firsthand account. If you have additional time for this unit, use Nardo's *Migrant Mother* or the Migrant Mother Web site to show students how history and real people intermingle.

Learning Activities
1. Invite students to embark on a solo investigation today. Students can select one primary source photograph from http://bit.ly/tsunami-links or browse one of the listed photography sites to find a new one.
2. After selecting a photo, students will work individually, drawing and filling in a fresh history detective chart.

Closure Invite students to share their thinking in pairs.

Assessment At the end of class period, students will submit their photo and chart for formative feedback.

DAY THREE (60 minutes): Background Check Research
Launching the Lesson: Activating Prior Knowledge
After handing back the previous days' student photos and graphic organizers with feedback, remind students that in order to know about these people's lives and what was happening then, a good detective does a background information check. So today, they will be doing background check research into the time period of their photograph.

Learning Activities
1. In the school library, students will utilize a Web site hotlist (see http://bit.ly/tsunami-links) and nonfiction print resources to gather facts about the time period. Students will use a wiki-based research graphic organizer to gather information—asking those detective-type questions—to determine and cite the background information for their first-person narrative. (See http://bit.ly/tsunami-links for links and a sample wiki template.)

2. Students will spend the entire class period conducting their investigation. The teacher and/or school librarian will be available to assist in the gathering of information.

Closure Ask students to begin to think about how this background information might form the setting for their first-person narrative and to brainstorm ideas for tomorrow.

DAY FOUR (60 minutes): First-Person Narrative
Launching the Lesson: Activating Prior Knowledge
The class will listen to short clips of personal narrative accounts of people from the Great Depression and Dust Bowl era (see http://bit.ly/tsunami-links). Ask students to listen for emotions such as despair, sadness, fear, hope, and/or urgency.

Learning Activities
1. Introduce the elements of a first-person narrative and the writing process steps that will be followed, according to the personal narrative graphic organizer you have selected. The background research will provide their setting, and the people in their photograph are their characters. It will be up to the students to put all the clues together to create a narrative that includes these elements along with what they think was happening in the photo, what the characters might be feeling, sensory details, a creative introduction, and an effective conclusion.
2. Students will use the remainder of class period for outlining and writing, with the teacher rotating to assist with feedback.

Closure Ask a few students to share one of their powerful details. Ask the students to finish their graphic organizer at home and begin writing their narratives. Tomorrow, they will continue writing and begin peer editing.

DAY FIVE (60 minutes): Writing and Editing
Launching the Lesson: Activating Prior Knowledge
1. Clarify the writing expectations for the class. Point out that narrative writing appeals to the audience's emotions while telling a story of an experience, an event, a list of recurring events, or a firsthand observable account. Write this information on the board or display it on-screen:

> Your personal narrative of your characters' Great Depression or Dust Bowl experience should tell your audience a story with:
> * an introduction
> * a well-planned story with a vivid description of the setting
> * a plot that explains what is happening to the audience and a conclusion
>
> Your narrative will also include:
> * factual information that reflects your knowledge about this time
> * sensory details (e.g., touch, feel, taste, sight, hearing)
> * your character's feelings and emotions

2. Distribute and discuss a copy of the rubric (page 85).

Learning Activities
Students will finish the first draft of their narratives.

Peer Assessment As students finish, the teacher will pair students up to review one another's work. Students will highlight strong writing and check the draft against the Personal Narrative Project Rubric (page 85). If extra time remains after peer editing, students can revise their work.

DAY SIX (60 minutes): Production Day
Launching the Lesson: Activating Prior Knowledge
As students enter the classroom, play the teacher's sample digital story. Ask students to identify strengths of the product that they can bring to their own project.

Learning Activities
1. Students will utilize computers to create their digital first-person narrative. Using a program of the teacher's choice (such as Animoto, VoiceThread, Microsoft Photo Story, PowerPoint's "Record Narration" feature, PrimaryAccess MovieMaker, VuVox, or Smilebox), students will insert the photograph (and perhaps additional primary sources) as they narrate their story. The teacher and school librarian will be available to assist students.
2. Students will then post stories to the class wiki.

Closure Invite students to visit the wiki and use the Discussion tab to leave supportive feedback for their colleagues.

Assessment Use the Personal Narrative Project Rubric (pages 85-86) both for student self-assessment and grading.

Extensions Ask students to reflect on their process. What would they do differently if they repeated this assignment with a different period in history? Alternatively, extend the writing experience beyond this "moment capture." What would happen to these characters if it rained? If they were offered the chance—or chose to—leave for other areas? What strangers might pass by, bringing news that would change their future? What might their lives be like a year in the future? Two years? See http://bit.ly/tsunami-links for additional extensions.

TSUNAMI TIP: Computer Captains
If you feel like you are being run ragged when you work in the computer lab or with laptops, consider assigning a computer captain to each row or table. When students have a question, they first ask the captain. This means the teacher will spend less time answering simple questions and more time on the more complex questions of comprehension and creation.

Rubric

Elements	5	3	1
Organization	The narrative has a clear sequence of events: beginning, middle, and end. It begins with the first, last, or most important event. It ends with the writer's feelings or thoughts about the experience.	The narrative may lack a clear beginning or end. It contains a personal comment or thought, but it may need more detail or explanation.	The narrative lacks a clear sequence of events. The writing does not have a beginning, middle, or end. It may lack any personal comment or reflection.
Narrative Elements	The narrative is interesting and has a clear point. The writer establishes a well-developed idea/plot and setting. The narrative contains specific factual details about people, places, and events; the details are appropriate for the intended audience. Provides meaningful insight into why the event/experience was memorable.	The narrative has a clear point. It contains some factual details about people, places, and events; some may not be identified clearly enough for the intended audience or reflect the time period. Provides little insight into why the event/experience was memorable.	The narrative may lack essential details. The amount and types of details do not demonstrate an awareness of the intended audience. There is a lack of factual details that indicate knowledge of the time period. Provides no insight into why the event/experience was memorable.
Point of View	The entire story is told from first-person point of view using the pronoun I.	The story is told from the writer's point of view, but may slip into other points of view and did not always use the pronoun I.	The story is not from the writer's point of view. The pronoun I is not used.
Sensory Details	Provides plenty of sensory details, creating a vivid picture and enabling the reader to visualize the events or experiences.	Has too few sensory details or far too many so the writing does not give a visual picture.	Paper is lacking in sensory details and tells rather than shows, using empty words.
Character Voice	The voice chosen clearly represents a figure in the photograph. The character has a unique voice, is from the Dust Bowl, and tells a story with a personal tone.	The character's voice may or may not represent a figure in the photograph. While the character mostly seems to be from the Dust Bowl era, there are some uncertain moments.	It is unclear that the character was inspired by a historical photograph. Also, the character's voice does not match the time period or have a personal point of view.

Continued on next page

From *Navigating the Information Tsunami: Engaging Research Projects That Meet the Common Core State Standards*, K-5. Cherry Lake Publishing, 2013.

Elements	5	3	1
Conventions	There are few or no errors in mechanics, usage, grammar, or spelling. Writing is punctuated correctly. Verb tense remains consistent.	There are several errors in mechanics, usage, grammar, or spelling. Writing is punctuated inconsistently. Word choice or spelling may hinder easy comprehension. Verb tenses are inconsistent throughout, affecting the reader's understanding.	Numerous errors in mechanics, usage, grammar, or spelling interfere with meaning. Writing may lack essential punctuation. Word choice or spelling may interfere with comprehension. Verb tenses are very inconsistent, making the paper difficult to understand.
Tone	The tone of the personal narrative matches that of the primary source photograph.	The tone of the personal narrative sometimes matches that of the photograph.	The tone is a mismatch for the photograph.
Primary Source Usage (Images)	Images selected are from the time period and have a person that is utilized as the main character of the narrative.	Images selected may be from the time period and have a person that is utilized as the main character of the narrative.	Images do not feature people and/or are not from the time period.
Resources and Bibliography	Used a wide variety of sources, both print and digital, to gather information and photographs. All the citations have the required elements. Provides citations for all images and sources utilized for research as a listing at the end of the narrative and/or at the end of their movie.	Used a limited variety of sources. Some the citations have the required elements. Provides citations for some of the sources and images utilized for research as a listing at the end of the narrative and/or at the end of their movie.	Only uses one type of source. The citations do not have all the required elements. There are very few or no citations for some of the sources and images utilized for research as a listing at the end of the narrative and/or at the end of their movie.

HOW DO WE STAY SAFE DURING LEISURE TIME?

Keywords: summer hobbies, safety, search engines, search strategies, Wikipedia, digital posters

Melissa P. Johnston and Kristin Fontichiaro

In fifth grade, students seek opportunities to prove themselves and to tackle additional responsibility for independent learning. This lesson gives them the chance to conduct research on a topic of interest and to create a meaningful resource to share with their friends. This digital safety flyer allows the students to independently choose a topic of interest, demonstrate open Web search strategies, and utilize their own creativity and technology skills to present their results in an engaging way.

Key Standards

Writing 5.7—Conduct short research projects that use several sources to build knowledge through investigation of different aspects of a topic.

Writing 5.8—Recall relevant information from experiences or gather relevant information from print and digital sources; summarize or paraphrase information in notes and finished work, and provide a list of sources.

To accomplish these standards, students will need to be able to

- keyboard with efficiency (Writing 5.6 sets a goal of two pages in one sitting);
- exercise choice and demonstrate self-confidence in selecting a topic of interest;
- employ effective search strategies to find and use quality Web sites and other digital resources;
- evaluate information found online;
- use multiple sources;
- value copyright and intellectual property rights of others;
- use technology to access, organize, and present information and understanding;
- create products that apply to authentic, real-world situations; and
- edit for conventions.

Time Needed

Three 60 minute sessions

Resource List

- ☑ Internet access
- ☑ Whiteboard/interactive whiteboard, projector, computer
- ☑ An account with Glogster.com or edu.Glogster.com (subscription)
- ☑ Sample Safety Glog to show students
- ☑ Glogster tutorials (see http://bit.ly/tsunami-links)
- ☑ Books on Web searching and Web site evaluation, which include activities:
  - *Find the Right Site* by Ann Truesdell (Cherry Lake, 2010)
  - *Find Your Way Online* by Suzy Rabbat (Cherry Lake, 2010)
- ☑ Summer Safety Search project sheet (page 90)
- ☑ Your school librarian, to teach search strategies, mini-conference with students, and be a second teacher

DAY ONE (60 minutes): Introduction and Search Strategies
Launching the Lesson: Activating Prior Knowledge

1. Before class, browse the airline safety cards at http://allsafetycards.com and select a card that represents an airline served by the closest airport. Display one using an opaque or data projector. You can also show Delta Airlines' in-flight safety video, found at www.youtube.com/watch?v = MgpzUo_kbFY (see page 72 if YouTube is blocked at school).

2. Ask students, "Why do airplanes require that we look at these cards or listen to these announcements? Why do they try to scare us when it's so much fun to fly? Aren't airplanes almost always safe?" In discussion, it is likely to come out that the cards and videos help people know what to do to stay safe when something goes wrong.

3. Now ask students to think of a few things they plan to do on their upcoming summer vacation. Invite volunteers to share an idea while one student (or the librarian) serves as recorder, writing them in a column on the whiteboard/interactive whiteboard. Then ask students if they can think of any hazards that they might encounter during each of these activities. Again, volunteers can share concerns while a student records their thinking in a second column. Ask, "Do we stop riding our bikes or waterskiing just because there can be an accident?" No, just like with airplanes, we know how to enjoy things safely.

Learning Activities

1. Review the list created by students and ask, "Wouldn't it be nice if you could help your friends know how to stay safe over the summer? Like at the beach when there are certain warning signs they put up to notify people of dangerous conditions?"

2. Explain that they will make a safety poster to share with their friends using Glogster, a digital poster-making site. Show students your sample glog.

3. Pass out the Summer Safety Search sheet (page 90). Explain that students will select a topic that interests them, use Web sites and databases to find information, evaluate information, and decide what to place on their glog.

4. Using the Tsunami Tip sheet from pp. 93-94, model a lesson on searching the open Web. Many elementary students have been using search engines like Bing or Google for many years but lack strategies beyond typing in a few words. In fact, many students search by typing in an entire question, which rarely leads to a reliable source.

5. Discuss how we determine if a site is of high quality. As a class, work with the librarian to do a search on the sample topic of airline safety. Pull up a few sites. Out of all the sites out there, is this site worth it? In the early days of the Web, we could rely on domain names or visual appearance to help us decide. But today, only .edu (educational sites, though these can include sites written by classes of young children) and .gov (governmental sites) are reliable indicators. Try the TRAPS mnemonic for evaluation:

TRAPS Web site Evaluation
Time: How recently was it written? A 12-year-old Web site about George Washington is probably still accurate, but a site about current events that is 12 years old? No way!
Readability: Is the site at our reading level? Do we understand most of it? Or is the vocabulary too difficult, making it hard to know what is being said?
Authority: Who wrote it? Are they experts? How can we tell? We might skim the major headings to help us decide.
Purpose: Why is the author writing the site? To inform? To persuade? That will help us know if what we have found is someone's opinion or fact.
Summary: All in all, is this a site worth spending time on? Or would it be better to look somewhere else?

Talk about the pros and cons of Wikipedia. Many students will want to use Wikipedia.com to search, even though most Wikipedia sites are longer and more complex than fifth graders can digest, and there are lingering concerns about the changeability of content. While Wikipedia is a comforting starting point for many students, help them see that real researchers might start there, but quickly move on to additional sites and sources. Let students know that most teachers and college professors don't want you to cite Wikipedia as a key source.

Wikipedia works great for
- finding basic information about a topic;
- getting some keywords or synonyms for future searches; and
- using the links at the bottom of the page to lead you to additional resources.

Wikipedia is not a great choice when
- it is the only source you rely on for a project; and
- there is information that is easier for you to read somewhere else.

6. Time to select a search and start searching! Using a wiki template (see http://bit.ly/tsunami-links) and/or the Summer Safety Glog sheet (page 90), students will take notes and list information they want to include on their poster.

Closure/Self-Assessment Ask students to partner and share what they have learned and identify places for additional research the following day.

DAY TWO (60 Minutes): Searching and Note Taking
Launching the Lesson: *Activating Prior Knowledge*
Ask students to remind you of some great strategies for searching the Web, evaluating a Web site, or using Wikipedia.

Learning Activities
Students will complete their searching and note taking today.

Closure Ask each student to share one tip with you before leaving the computer lab.

Assessment Ask students to turn in their notes so you can check for progress and understanding.

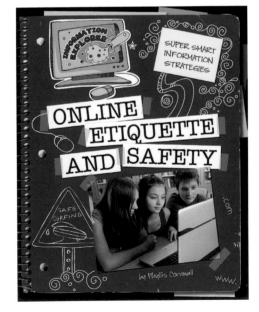

Summer Safety Search

Choose Your Topic! Beach Safety – Biking Safety – Boating Safety – Camping Safety –
Car/Auto Safety – Hiking Safety – Internet Safety – Playground/Park Safety –
Severe Summer Weather Safety – Sun Safety – Swimming/Diving Safety – _____ Safety

You will create a "Dos and Don'ts" digital poster for your classmates. You will need to do research in these areas*:

Think About…	Sample Notes (for Airline Safety)	Your Notes
How to prepare ahead of time—precautionary measures: What equipment is needed? What do you need to pack?	• Check www.TSA.gov • Carry-on toiletries 3 oz or less, in clear zippered bag • Photo ID	
Protective measures	• Airline cancels if weather is bad. Air marshals on plane. Security gates. Flight attendants point out exits & give safety tips. • Can't take weapons on plane.	
What to wear	• Slip-on shoes for security. No jewelry, belts, jackets at security.	
Dangers/hazards	• Bad weather • Mechanical failure • Terrorism	
What would you put in a first aid kit?	• Nothing—flotation cushions, first aid, oxygen masks on board	
What do you do if you get hurt?	• Tell flight attendant. Listen for directions.	

*Remember to cite your sources on the back!

DAY THREE (60 Minutes): Creating the Digital Poster
Launching the Lesson: Activating Prior Knowledge

Begin by showing students a brief Glogster video tutorial (see http://bit.ly/tsunami-links). Encourage students to ask questions; pause the video if needed. Consider posting the videos on your class wiki so that students can refer to them later.

Learning Activities

1. Return the students' notes, along with your comments, to the class. The students will use their notes, computers, and Glogster to create their Glogs according to the assessment sheet (page 92). Glogster allows them to type in text but also embed audio, video, or images. Remind students that all text should be their own. They may use multimedia from another source, but it must be cited in a caption, because great researchers give great credit to others' work! When using Glogster for a school project, it is important that students do more than just assemble others' materials. Ask, "If I took everybody else's work away—the videos you embedded, the websites you linked to, or the photos you used—what would be left that is your work?" Continuously push beyond mere scrapbooking of others' work!

2. Students will work independently while the teacher and/or school librarian will rotate around to each group to answer questions, give formative feedback, and evoke discussion if needed.

3. This same procedure may be repeated for an additional day if there are students who take longer to finish.

Closure Students will save, name, and embed their glog on the class wiki. Other students in the class will view glogs and choose two to comment on using the class's Discussion tab.

Assessment Ask students to reflect and evaluate their work according to the checklist (page 92), and use the same checklist to provide them with a final grade.

Extensions Share the class's work with younger students by hosting a poster session in the classroom, hallway, multipurpose room, or library.

TSUNAMI TIP: Giving Credit in a Multimedia World

There are many online tools that make it easy to mash up other people's text, videos, audio, and photos. Many children equate the *availability* of multimedia content with implicit permission to take it as their own. This builds poor career and college habits and makes it difficult for you to trace their work back to its sources.

How do we help students respect others' ownership rights? To begin, remind students that *their* work is protected by copyright, as is the work of everyone in their class, family, and neighborhood, unless they have given other permission. Secondly, be sure, as this assignment shows, to save space in a product to give, at the minimum, the title, author, and, if a digital work, URL.

Self-Assessment

☐ The project addresses each item on the project sheet.

☐ Someone using my glog would know how to be safe doing the activity.

☐ My project uses reassuring language and does not scare people.

☐ The project uses outstanding resources.

☐ Visual elements match the tone of the glog.

☐ Multimedia elements enhance the message. They do more than just decorate the page.

☐ Each multimedia element is cited beneath the resource.

☐ A works cited list is included.

☐ I used my time wisely.

☐ I completed my project on time.

☐ I did my best work.

The overall quality of my process was:

☐ outstanding   ☐ very good   ☐ good   ☐ fair   ☐ poor

The overall quality of the project is:

☐ outstanding   ☐ very good   ☐ good   ☐ fair   ☐ poor

I grew as a researcher during this project because I got better at

_____ .

If I were going to do this project again, I would work on improving my skills in _____

_____ .

From Navigating the Information Tsunami: Engaging Research Projects That Meet the Common Core State Standards, K-5. Cherry Lake Publishing, 2013.

GRADE 5

TSUNAMI TIP: Be a Better Searcher

Tasha Bergson-Michelson

Searching for information is like being a detective. When we write down words that we would type into a search engine like Google, we show the words in brackets, like this: [thanksgiving myths]. The brackets do not get typed in; they just remind us of the search box.

Did you know that there are some searches that work better than others? If you want to go above basic detective and become a searching sleuth, follow these tips!

When you sleuth for information, start with a few, specific words to describe the main idea of what you want. Skip capital letters. For example, you may type [recycling center], [george washington biography], [playground safety], or [igneous rocks]. Let's say that you are just starting a research project about Vikings, so you search for [vikings].

When you type in Vikings, what do you expect to see?

Carefully read your results for clues. Pay special attention to the words in bold. Those are the words that Google matches to your needs.

Think carefully about whether your results
1. match what you expected to find;
2. have unexpected results that you can fix; or
3. offer any words or new ideas that you can incorporate into your next search.

Sometimes, as you practice on your way to becoming a supersleuth, it is a good idea to print out a page of results and write on them to help you really think about what your results are telling you.

For more information, visit the Search Education Web site: http://www.google.com /insidesearch/searcheducation/

These are some common challenges that might cause you to get information different than what you expected—and some suggestions for how to solve them.

Problem	Solution
The pages I found are too casual for schoolwork or they are too hard to read.	Make sure the words you type in match the level of formality or difficulty you need. For example, which of these words best match what you need: cop, police, or officer?
The idea I am looking for can be said or spelled in a few different ways.	First, look at your results and see if Google is already looking for the synonyms you have in mind. The words Google is using to find your pages are in bold in your results. If Google has not automatically searched for a synonym, add it to your search with OR, in all capital letters. Example: [mohican OR mahican]
The information I need might be in a picture, book, map, or video, not a regular Web page.	Check Google Images, Google Books, Google Maps, or Google Videos by clicking on those choices in the column to the left side of your search results.
I wanted words together in a phrase, but they are not together in the results.	Put quotation marks around the words that you want to keep together in a phrase. For example, finding someone named ["Thomas Jefferson Franklin"] will stop results for pages about Benjamin Franklin or even Thomas Franklin and only give you results with all three words, in order.
My results suggest that there might be another search term I can use.	If you see a word you don't know, do a search for [define:word] to find out what it means. If it is a good word to express your idea, try using it in a search. For example, if you search for [vikings], you might see the word Norse in some results. Searching [vikings norse] will get rid of results about the football team.
I just want information from a specific point in time.	Look to the left of your search results. Near the bottom of that column on the left, there is a link that says "More search tools." Click to expand that column, and click on one of the links to limit the search by the age of the Web page.
My results are not relevant because the word I want has another use, too.	Use a minus sign (-) in front of the word that you want to get rid of from your results. Do not put a space between the minus sign and the word that follows. If you are interested in the historical Vikings, but not the Minnesota Vikings, try [vikings -minnesota].
I really like this one Web site. Does it have other good pages?	Use a "site:" search to tell Google to look in just one place. Example: [aztecs site:nationalgeographic.com] is a search that will only look on the National Geographic site to find information.
I typed a question into the Google search box and got a lot of Q&A sites, which my teacher said I shouldn't use for homework.	Typing a question will not bring you the best results. Try to type only the keywords. To learn how, visit http://mindshift.kqed.org/2012/02/how-to-choose-the-right-words-for-best-search-results!

About the Contributors

Tasha Bergson-Michelson is on the Search Education team at Google and founder, research skills consultant and trainer at To The Point Research.

Jan Dohner is a librarian, researcher, and author of nonfiction. She is currently working at Maltby Intermediate and Scranton Middle Schools in Brighton, Michigan, where she also serves as the English Language Arts coordinator. She is the author of *The Encyclopedia of Historic and Endangered Livestock and Poultry Breeds* (Yale, 2001), *Livestock Guardians: Using Dogs, Donkeys and Llamas to Protect Your Herd* (Storey, 2007), and various articles.

Kristin Fontichiaro teaches in the University of Michigan Schools of Information and Education. Beyond her books for Cherry Lake, she is the author of *Podcasting at School* (Libraries Unlimited, 2008) and coauthor of *Story Starters and Science Notebooking: Developing Student Thinking Through Literacy and Inquiry* (Teacher Ideas Press, 2009), among others. She can be reached at font@umich.edu.

Kara Fribley is a graduate of the University of Michigan School of Information and author of *Find the Right Words with Thesauruses* (Cherry Lake, 2012).

Jenny Harner is a National Board Certified Teacher working at Rising Sun Elementary in the Cecil County (Maryland) Public Schools. She can be reached at http://ccps.org/teachers/JLHarner.

Emily Johnson is the librarian at Pledge Harbor Sports Academy in Dhaka, Bangladesh. A graduate of the University of Michigan School of Information, she is coauthor of the forthcoming Cherry Lake title *Know What to Ask: Forming Great Research Questions*. Contact her at emily.johnson314@gmail.com.

Melissa P. Johnston, PhD, is an assistant professor at the School of Library and Information Studies at the University of Alabama. Before earning her doctorate at Florida State University, Melissa taught at the elementary school level for 12 years. She can be reached at mpjohnston@slis.ua.edu.

Linda Martin teaches at Sugar Hill Elementary in Gainesville, Georgia. She is a storyteller and the author of *The Story Bracelet Manual* (QOTL Productions, 2007). She can be reached at lindamartin423@gmail.com.

Ann O'Keefe teaches at King and Pittsfield Elementaries in the Ann Arbor (Michigan) Public Schools. She can be reached at annokeefe4@gmail.com.

Andy Plemmons teaches at David C. Barrow Elementary in Athens, Georgia. He can be reached at plemmonsa@clarke.k12.ga.us or at http://barrowmediacenter.wordpress.com.

Suzy Rabbat is a National Board-Certified Teacher and a school library media consultant in the Chicago area. She created the concept for Cherry Lake's Information Explorers series and authored several books in the series. She can be reached at suzyrabbat@gmail.com.

Eileen Thomas teaches at Lakewood Elementary in the Ann Arbor (Michigan) Public Schools.

Ann Truesdell teaches in Birmingham, Michigan. She has written six titles for Cherry Lake's Information Explorer and Information Explorer Junior series. Ann loves history, traveling, and spending time with her husband, Mike, and their children, James and Charlotte.

Sara Wilkie teaches and learns with a fifth/sixth grade multiage class in Birmingham, Michigan. She taught for 13 years before adding the roles of learning mentor and professional development coach to her repertoire. Sara coauthored *Team Up Online* and is the author of *Social Studies Projects That Shine*, both part of Cherry Lake's Information Explorers series.

Looking for More Lessons Like These?

If this book's lessons leave you yearning for more, consider Cherry Lake's books for K-8 learners. Today's kids need a robust toolkit for the 21st century. Cherry Lake Publishing partners with educators and experts to bring vibrant, active learning experiences to print and eBooks for K-8 learners. Our books blend informational text with engaging activities that work for a single student -- or your entire class!

Shooting Video to Make Learning Fun

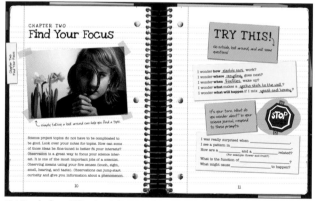

Get Ready for a Winning Science Project

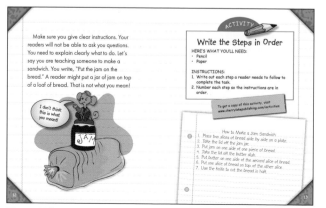

How to Write a How-To

In our Information Explorer series for upper elementary and middle school students, we unpack the digital and information literacy skills students need to read, write, research, and share in a transliterate, multimedia world. From a student's first questions to the final science fair display, from outline to podcast, from primary source to social studies projects, each book blends informational text with five hands-on application activities.

For younger students, the companion Information Explorer Junior series gives an initial introduction to digital and print literacies for the lower elementary learner.

The Language Arts Explorer series applies the NCTE/IRA Standards to science and social studies content. Each book sends the reader on a fact-finding mission, posing an initial challenge and concluding with questions and answers. Through engaging, interactive scenarios, learners can experiment with text prediction, purpose-driven research, and creative problem solving.

Language Arts Explorer Junior series gives an easy-to-read introduction to writing across the genres, including how-to books, book reports, and more.

Preview our titles and learn more at *cherrylakepublishing.com*.